Contents

Introduction

To a child the natural world is full of wonder and excitement. Adults must, of course, be mindful of complex environmental issues but at the same time maintain a child-like inquisitiveness. Through outdoor play and exploring the wild comes a desire for knowledge that gives real meaning to the facts of natural science. It is not a crime for an adult to be unable to name a flower or bird, but a shared learning opportunity for young and old.

As a mother of six, I'm well versed in the barriers that today's society puts in the way of spending time out of doors with children. Richard Louv in his book *Last Child in the Woods: Saving Our Children from Nature-Deficit Disorder* argues that sensationalist media coverage and paranoid parents have scared children away from woods and fields.

In my opinion, the opportunity for getting out and doing the wild stuff has to be realistic and local. After-school sports expend energy—and this is important in a world where too many children are clinically obese—but it's not the same as natural, unstructured, out-of-doors play. Our world is filled with stranger-danger rules, which purport to make a child safe. My siblings and I were allowed to take risks, enjoying a freedom that often presented the unexpected such as a bull in a field. The rules

of nature's playground are unstructured and yet call for immediacy and sensibility. Solitude is free and sometimes necessary for a naturalist. It is, however, often lacking in a world of sleep-deprived teenagers keeping up with the demands of social media.

Young children are easily persuaded to "come outside." Kicking leaves, splashing in puddles, and cooking with foraged ingredients are all tempting. Older children—or those who are not outdoor types—may need some coaxing. Carers can always find chores to do, but you may also benefit from daily interaction with nature and a teen. Try a 5-minute excursion into the garden to identify the birds or a walk around the block to spot different plants and flowers. Outdoor friendships will grow as you share thoughts about the natural world.

Our forefathers were in touch with the rhythm of the seasons, but modern life has sadly cut us off from such close contact with nature. An understanding of our natural world links you closely with your grandparents and generations before them. This doesn't mean young naturalists can't be techie too, though. Digital cameras are amazing; they can be used to capture wild plants and animals in an instant. Geocaching is a modern treasure hunt activity that uses GPS (Global Positioning System). Seekers are directed toward small stashes of treasure in urban and rural spots. Once there, the geocachers record the visit in the log book (or online) and take and replace small trinkets of treasure. On another day you might want to spend time in the wild on your own and simply be still and quiet.

A Basic Wild Knapsack

Here is a list of useful items for wild adventures. Before you set off, think about the type of environment you're visiting and take all the things you may need, so you can get the most out of your wild experience.

★ Bottle of water

★ Scissors

★ Penknife

★ Hand pruners/secateurs (older children)

★ Double-sided tape

★ String and thread

★ Magnifying glass

★ Pocket-sized I.D. book

★ First aid kit (including band-aids, antiseptic wipes, and insect repellent)

★ Cellphone/mobile phone (for useful apps and safety)

★ Camera

★ Snap-and-seal bags

★ Small plastic containers with lids (a short-stay bug home—you can never have too many of these)

★ Small wind-up flashlight/torch (for looking into cracks and rock-pooling)

★ Notepad (make a habit of writing up your discoveries)

★ Pencil (this won't blot if it gets wet)

★ Small paintbrush

★ Old spoon

★ Small sieve

★ Bucket (for pond dipping and rock-pooling)

★ Tape measure

★ Tweezers

★ Bin liner (make a head hole for a waterproof or use it for any garbage)

Summer
★ Sunscreen and sun hat

Winter
★ Warm hat and washable gloves

Useful Extras

Being a naturalist is not expensive. Nature is there for everyone to enjoy—there isn't an entry charge. If, however, you enjoy looking at plants and wildlife, and cooking with wild ingredients, you may find this list of additional items helpful:

★ Waterproof camera (although expensive, a photograph captures plants, seaweed, and wildlife without disturbing the environment)

★ Waterproof binoculars

★ Telescope

★ Microscope

★ Food dehydrator (for drying blossom, leaves, berries, and seaweed)

★ Digital scales for accurately weighing seaweed, petals, and other dried ingredients (dried ingredients are light in weight)

★ Blotting paper

★ Scrapbooks

The Right Clothes

Wear the right clothes for the habitat you're exploring and pack to keep yourself safe. Here are some tips:

★ Make sure you have a warm sweater and a wrap-away waterproof jacket.

★ A lightweight buff is really useful because it can be used as a hat as well as a neck warmer.

★ If it's hot, keep out of the midday sun. Wear cotton clothing and where it is safe, jump in water to cool off.

★ Wear layers—it is much better to be too warm than too cold. Layers can be peeled off.

★ A wetsuit is useful if you're spending time in wetlands or by the seashore.

★ Dress: camouflage yourself and choose nature's colors. Greens and browns, not neon red, are nature's choices.

★ Wear strong and suitable footwear.

Safety First

Be safe and mindful when you are exploring and playing outside. NOTE TO CARERS: Whether working on projects indoors or outside, children should be supervised and helped where necessary, depending on their practical abilities.

★ Always ask an adult to go to wild places with you.

★ I.D. is the wild kids' code word for identification. Don't pick or eat anything unless you are absolutely sure you know what it is.

★ Cooking poisonous plants does not make them safe.

★ Always wash your hands after handling things in the wild and especially well after touching bones and animal droppings.

★ Don't pick plants that are protected by government law (see page 124).

★ Don't pull up plant roots.

★ When foraging, don't be greedy—pick a little here and there.

★ Pick wild salad leaves slowly and I.D. each leaf with care, ensuring you don't pick different species that may be growing nearby—these may be dangerous.

★ Be alert to fire, snakes, and ticks. Ticks are a nuisance and can cause Lyme disease.

★ Keep pets under control and respect livestock. Keep your distance from cattle with calves.

★ Keep to paths when asked to do so and shut gates. Don't damage hedges, walls, or fences.

★ Care for the countryside—leave no more than a footprint.

Plants to I.D. and Avoid

Nature provides free food and medicines, but we need to learn how to I.D. plants correctly. Each of us has different tolerances when we touch plants and the contact time for a bad reaction can vary from person to person. Young naturalists must learn about harmful as well as edible plants. Make a list of poisonous plants to look out for in your neighborhood. Your local environmental agency will give you helpful advice.

Wild poisons

★ Castor bean plant (*Ricinus communis*)

★ Deadly nightshade (*Atropa belladonna*) If you eat the leaves and/or berries of this plant, you can die. This is why it is called deadly.

★ Foxgloves (*Digitalis* spp.) If you know someone with a heart condition, you may recognize this plant's Latin name because the leaves are used in the heart drug digitalis. Although some poisonous plants are used in medicines, this does not mean that you can eat them.

★ Hemlock (*Conium maculatum*) The philosopher Socrates was given a cup of poisonous hemlock juice to drink after his trial—he died as a result. This is a plant to learn to I.D. and then avoid.

★ The red berries of Jack in the pulpit (*Arum maculatum*)—also known as cuckoo pint or lords and ladies—are pretty but poisonous. This plant sometimes grows near wild garlic, so make sure you don't pick a handful in error. All parts are toxic.

★ Mistletoe (*Phoradendron*/USA and *Viscum album*/UK); American poison ivy (*Toxicodendron* spp.); British ivy (*Hedera helix*); and yew (*Taxus baccata*) are all poisonous. Yew is one of the deadliest trees in the world. The berries and leaves of some of these plants are used for Christmas decorations and, although birds enjoy eating these berries, humans must not. Always wash your hands after touching any flora or fauna.

Other plants to look out for

★ Giant hogweed (*Heracleum sphondylium*) can grow to enormous heights—much taller than an adult. If its sap comes in contact with your skin, it can burn and leave you with horrid blisters.

★ Be wary of bushes with thorns and trees with needles. Thorns from wild roses and blackberry bushes, as well as sharp pine needles, can cause infection if they aren't removed quickly.

★ Avoid ragwort (*Jacobaea vulgaris*) if you suffer from allergies or asthma. It is poisonous to horses. Scots call ragwort stinking Willie after William Duke of Cumberland who led the loyalists at the Battle of Culloden against Bonnie Prince Charlie and the Jacobites—the battle path was covered with ragwort.

Unlucky plants

★ Blackthorn (*Prunus spinosa*) Country people refused to bring blackthorn into the house as it was considered a bad omen—usually indicating that somebody would die.

★ Holly (*Ilex aquifolium*) It was said to be unlucky to hang this evergreen over mirrors at Christmastime.

★ Mistletoe It was thought unlucky to bring mistletoe indoors before Christmas Eve.

★ All decorations, including holly and mistletoe, had to be taken down before Old Christmas Day (or Twelfth Night)—or it was believed that the "Devil would dance on every spray."

The Activities

1 Hear the Sound of Silence

Go out into the wild: sit down, listen, watch, smell the air, and be still. Sense the seasons. Write down what you see, smell, and hear. Then tap your head and become yourself again!

2 Fly a Plastic Kite

This carrier-bag kite doesn't have a frame, so it is quick and simple to make. If you are a good beachcomber, you may even find some abandoned string on the beach or the seaweed dead man's rope. Take a long piece of string or seaweed, tie one end securely to a twig (or a kelp stipe), measuring about 10in (25cm) in length, and wind the string or seaweed neatly around the twig or kelp stipe. Tie the other end of the string or seaweed to the handles of the carrier bag.

Run, catch the wind in the bag, and let the string out as your kite lifts in the wind.

3 Go on a Leaf Hunt

When exploring the woods, see how many different leaves you can spot. Here are some tips for identifying the leaves you've found:

➡ Touch a leaf and feel its texture—is it glossy, rough, smooth, hairy, or downy?

➡ Collect and stick different types of leaf on both sides of some double-sided sticky tape and then I.D. the trees that the leaves have come from. In season, the flowers and fruits (or nuts, which are fruits in a hard case) will also help you to name the tree.

➡ You could hang the leaf strips over a branch or loop and fasten a small strip to create a woodland head-dress. Stick small pieces of fern or fir between the colorful leaves to add some greenery if you wish.

➡ A pocket tree guide or phone app will help you confirm a tree's I.D.

4 Make an Octopus

This project is a great way to use a plastic bottle. It is very easy to make, but adult supervision may be required. Dried pom pom weed, carrageen, or beach sponge are perfect for the hair.

What you need

- ★ Scissors
- ★ 17fl oz (500ml) clean plastic bottle
- ★ Knife with a pointed end
- ★ 3 lengths of craft cord, one measuring 28in (70cm) and two measuring ¾–1¼in (2–3cm)
- ★ Dinner candle in a suitable holder (e.g. a glass bottle)
- ★ Pair of googly eyes
- ★ Nail polish
- ★ Craft glue
- ★ Dried pom pom weed, carrageen, or beach sponge
- ★ 2 pieces of dried dulse or bladder wrack, 6in (15cm) in length

1   Use the scissors to cut the top off the plastic bottle. Turn the bottle upside down and use the pointed knife to make a hole (large enough for threading the craft cord through) in the middle of the bottom of the bottle.

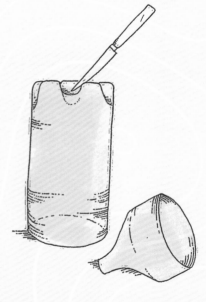

2   Use the scissors to cut strips in the open end of the bottle—these are the octopus's tentacles—leaving about 1½–2in (4–5cm) of plastic at the base for the octopus's head.

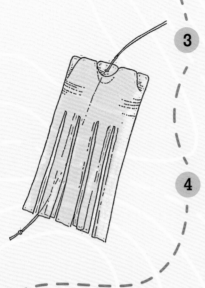

3 Thread the longer piece of craft cord through the hole in the bottom of the bottle (the head) and tie a big knot in the end so that you'll be able to hang up your octopus.

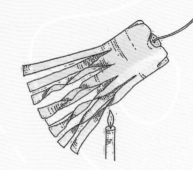

4 Light the candle and then create the wavy tentacles by twisting the strips over the flame to melt the plastic. Be careful, but quick, or the plastic may go black.

5 Stick on the googly eyes and add extra details with the nail polish.

6 Glue the dried pom pom weed, carrageen, or sponge to the top of the bottle to create the hair, and leave to dry.

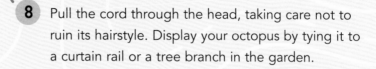

7 Take the longer piece of craft cord and use the two shorter lengths of cord to tie the pieces of dulse or bladder wrack just above the knot so that the seaweed hangs down the middle. The color of the seaweed will fade over time.

8 Pull the cord through the head, taking care not to ruin its hairstyle. Display your octopus by tying it to a curtain rail or a tree branch in the garden.

5 Spot these Woodland Trees

Look for different plants through the seasons, such as winter snowdrops and spring bluebells, as well as broadleaved trees that shed their leaves in the fall (autumn) and have flowers that develop into fruits. Coniferous trees produce seeds inside cones.

The wild cherry has flowers that hang in clusters and are an early source of nectar for visiting bees. The birds enjoy eating its fruit— perhaps this is why it's sometimes called the sweet bird cherry. In Scotland it is called the gean. Small mammals (at ground level) enjoy eating fallen wild cherries too.

The elder roots with ease and grows with speed. It fills gaps in hedgerows and, given the chance, bushes into woods too, but it's a spindly tree. Elderflower blossom is honey-scented and a favorite with nectar-gathering honeybees. You can use the blossom to make elderflower syrup. In fall (autumn), the Lilliputian berries are just the right size for a fairy's table or you can use them to make syrups or jams. These berries are rich in Vitamin C, but you may need to add sugar if you cook with them. Use a stick to pull down high branches to pick the blossom and berries.

The crab apple is a beautiful tree with spring blossom that attracts bees and lots of other flying insects. Robins, starlings, greenfinches, and thrushes are particularly fond of its tiny apples in the fall (autumn). Don't bite into these apples, though—they are tart and best taken into your wild kitchen. They are packed with pectin, which helps jams and jellies to set. The crab apple tree is common in cities and parkland too.

The sycamore Sycamores grow in the shade; in fact, they aren't fussy where they grow. In the United Kingdom, where the sycamore is non-native, people who disliked the tree used to hold "syccie bashing" events to remove this invasive tree. Indeed, some conservationists worry that alien species are ecologically harmful. However, non-native species that aren't damaging natural species can sometimes help us out, especially when native species become diseased. The familiar sycamore keys, which are such fun to watch as they flutter and spiral to the ground in the fall (autumn), are formed from a cluster of olive flowers that are pollinated by insects.

6 Spot these Woodland Plants

Spring is the best time to look for woodland flowers before the ferns and nettles grow too high. See how many of the following you can spot on walks throughout the year.

Wood sorrel flowers in woods in mid- to late spring. This little white flower is a helpful weathervane, closing its petals at the first hint of any rain. On sunny days it will help you keep track of the time because its petals close as it starts to go dark. The pretty, heart-shaped leaves look like clover but taste of lemon. You can use both wood sorrel and sheep sorrel to give a lemon flavor in cooking.

Woodruff is another white spring woodland flower. Confusingly, although "odor" appears in its Latin name, it doesn't have a strong scent. However, there is a scented clue in one of its local names: sweet scented bedstraw. This is because dried woodruff (unlike fresh) is scented thanks to a chemical called coumarin. In the past, woodruff was used to scent rooms and linen, just as we use lavender and roses today. Pick woodruff from mid- to late spring, tie it in a bunch, and leave to dry. It will scent a room and keep moths away.

Snowdrops Galanthophiles are snowdrop lovers and some snowdrop varieties are much sought after. In the United Kingdom, in February 2015, a snowdrop fan paid US$2,120 (£1,390) for a *Galanthus plicatus* bulb. There are hundreds of hybrid snowdrops, most of which grow in gardens and churchyards, but some carpet woods from mid-winter to early spring.

Wild garlic You might smell ramsons or wild garlic before you see them. Like bluebells, they carpet damp woodland and moist banks. Use the flowers and leaves to give a garlic flavor in cooking. Pick a leaf, squeeze it in your hand, and you will smell garlic.

Bluebells are native to British woods, but are sadly under threat from the invasive Spanish bluebell. A walk in a native bluebell wood is something any child or adult living in or visiting the United Kingdom should do in spring.

Horsetails reproduce using spores rather than seeds—like their close relatives, the ferns. The first stems appear in spring and are topped with brown, cone-like structures that bear the spores. Later in the year, you'll see larger stems with tough, stringy leaves that give the plant its feathery, horsetail appearance. Horsetails spread quickly—in fact, they are considered invasive in some areas. Horsetails are living fossils, being the only surviving members of the class Equisetopsida. For more than a 100 million years, Equisetopsida plants, stretching up to 98ft (30m) high, dominated forest floors of the late Mesozoic period (254–65 million years ago).

Bilberries are tiny, but delicious. These plants grow on moors and in mature woods—look for the greenish-pink flowers in spring and pick the dark blue fruit in late summer. Bilberries may be called huckleberries or whortleberries but, whatever the name, they're not blueberries. They are, however, just the right size for grazing on. You'll have to be quick, though, because insects, birds, rodents, and deer like them too. The juice stains fingers and you may find yourself with a bilberry moustache. Not surprisingly, the berries were once used as a dye (see pages 63–64 to learn how to dye a handkerchief).

Make a Woodland Broom

7

This type of broom is called a besom. Traditionally, the handle is made from hazel branches and the head from birch twigs, but you can use whatever you find when exploring the woods. Just check that the broom will fit the witch or wizard it's being made for. Try to find a smooth handle that doesn't have any knobbles.

What you need

★ Penknife and/or potato peeler

★ A long stick (about the thickness of a broom handle)

★ Garden plant wire

★ Lots of thin twigs, about 14in (35cm) in length and ½in (1cm) in diameter

★ Strong string

1 Use the penknife or potato peeler to smooth away any knobbles or tiny branches on the stick (the broom handle). If you wish, you can carefully strip away the bark to make the stick smooth, or leave the bark on so that your broom has character.

2 Lay the stick on the ground and slip a length of plant wire under the bottom at the point where you want to tie the twigs to the broom to make the brush.

3 Weave the wire around each of the twigs as you attach them to the broom handle. When you have enough twigs in place on the first side, wind the wire around the handle to secure the twigs.

4 Turn the broom over and repeat the process on the other side. You can add more layers of twigs to each side to make a thicker brush if you wish.

5 When you have completed the layers, wind some string very tightly around the finished brush. It's a good idea to wind the string round lots of times to produce a cordage collar. This will look neat and also help secure the twigs firmly to the handle. Tie the string as tightly as you can.

6 You are now ready to sweep the leaves from your wigwam or den floor.

TIP

If you are making the broom at home, rather than in the woods, you can achieve a neater and stronger finish by sticking some carpet tape on top of the string around the broom handle. Then wrap a strip of burlap (hessian) sacking over the tape—ensuring it's wide enough to hide the tape and long enough to wrap twice around the twigs—and tie it in a bow.

8 Tell the Age of a Tree

When a tree has died or been cut down, you can look at the growth rings in an open section of trunk and age the tree. Each band is made up of two rings: a lighter ring (the spring growth) and a darker band (the late-summer growth). The older rings are closest to the center of the tree. The ring sizes may differ but this doesn't matter; it still counts as a year of the tree's life. A wide ring means the tree grew well that year and a narrower ring that its growth was stunted. For example, the rings will be thicker in wet and warmer years, but narrower in years when rainfall is low.

A tree's growth can also be affected by snow, levels of sunlight, and temperature, as well as how crowded it is by other trees. Studying the rings (ideally, with a magnifying glass) will tell you a lot about a tree's growth. The wind can also shape trees—you can see this on windswept hills, where a prevailing wind has dried out the new growth buds on one side.

Dendrochronology is the study of change through tree ring growth. You can also estimate the age of a pine tree by counting the whorls where the branches have grown out.

9 Go Tree Hugging

Find a tree you can reach all the way round with your arms and give it a hug. Or, perhaps find a bigger tree and link arms with friends to hug the tree.

10 Play Tree Tag

Have a fun game of tag in the woods and choose a special tree to be home. Run from the chaser, touch the tree, and you are safe.

11 Go Tree Bark Rubbing

You can make your own bark rubbings and write personal messages on these if you wish. Future generations will be able to read your thoughts if you stick the labeled rubbings in a scrapbook. You will need some sheets of white paper, wax crayons, and sticky tape. Simply hold a piece of white paper against a tree (or tape the paper to the trunk) as you color with a wax crayon. The ridges and bumps of the bark will appear on your paper. Crayon gently, especially over big knobbles in the bark. Collect rubbings from different tree species. Name the tree, date the rubbings, and then mount them in a scrapbook or keep them in a poly-pocket file.

12 Make a Dream Catcher

Native Americans made dream catchers to protect them from bad dreams while they slept. Good dreams would pass through the hole in the center of the dream catcher and slip down the feathers to the person sleeping below. The feather meant life or a breath of air. The type of feather used was important. An owl's feather was for wisdom and an eagle's for courage. The Native Americans would have woven natural thread (see *Make Nettle String*, on page 58) across the circle to catch the bad dreams. The bad dreams were trapped in the web and disappeared at dawn.

13 Make a Miniature Den and Garden

Build a miniature den and garden, perhaps for a stick person to live in (see *Make a Teasel Wizard*, on page 53). Build the den using twigs and, for ease, use a tree trunk as a back-supporting wall. Use twigs, bark, leaves, nuts, hips, haws, cones, mosses, ferns, lichen, burs, conker cases, and horsetails to create little homes and gardens. Just look around for inspiration. Here are some ideas for using the things you find:

★ Lay twigs on the ground to make decking and paths. Use fir cones as trees or hedging and use cleavers, honeysuckle, acorns, conkers, and burs for fences.

★ Use some grass or moss to make an instant lawn.

★ Use horsetails and fern leaflets (from a frond) as mini trees and cut common wild flowers and bright berries to create some pretty flowerbeds.

14 Make a Woodland Star

Sticks and string and a few wild treasures are transformed into this decorative star to hang from a tree.

1. Lay three sticks on the ground in the shape of a triangle, with the ends overlapping, and use small lengths of string to tie them together.

2. Repeat to make a second triangle with the remaining sticks. Place one triangle on top of the other so that it looks like a star.

3. Tie the two triangles tightly together with some more string to make the star.

4. Tie a length of string at the top of the star so that you can hang it from a tree.

5. Hang two or three lengths of sticky tape from the bottom of the star.

6. Use your imagination to decorate the star by attaching wild treasures, such as leaves, twigs, and seeds, to the frame and also sticking some "wildness" to the sticky tape. Don't use anything too heavy (e.g. a very big fir cone).

What you need

★ 6 dry sticks, about 12in (30cm) in length

★ String

★ Scissors

★ Double-sided sticky tape

★ Wild treasures

15 Build a Woodland Wigwam

Create a private den near your favorite tree and have fun creating a little home of your own in the woods. You can use your den as a hideout while you watch and study woodland wildlife.

What you need

★ A tree in a glade
★ Fallen branches (e.g. from beech and birch trees)
★ Logs and/or large stones
★ Rope and/or string
★ Scissors or a penknife
★ Twigs
★ Ferns
★ Moss, heather, or dried leaves (depending on the season)

(1) Find a tree standing alone in a glade. Other trees are fine, but a stand-alone tree will give you more space to work in.

(2) Search for large branches to lean against the trunk of the tree. It is better to use several thinner branches, if possible, than a smaller number of bigger branches as they will be easier to maneuver. Also look out for logs or stones to put at the base of the branches to hold them in place.

(3) Use rope or string to tie the branches individually to the tree. You can also tie the branches to each other, but the wigwam will be more stable—and less likely to collapse—if each branch is tied individually. You can use the spider's web of string created when tying on the branches to support the ferns later on.

(4) Now that you have the basic structure, start weaving twigs between the branches, particularly at the base. You can use some string to help you here too.

(5) Begin to fill in all of the gaps with dense layers of fern.

(6) Use moss, heather, ferns, or leaves to cover the floor of the wigwam and place logs inside to sit on.

16 Make a Catapult

Y ou can have lots of fun in the woods with a catapult. Hazel trees provide the strongest wood for catapults, so look for these when you're hunting for a Y-shaped piece of wood. Crab apple wood is also a good choice. Remember never to fire your catapult at any living thing. This is an adaptation of the author Abi Elphinstone's guide to making a catapult.

What you need

★ Penknife and/or potato peeler
★ Garden cutters (optional)
★ 2 large rubber bands
★ Y-shaped piece of wood
★ Fir cones (for firing)

TIP

When you get home, you can strengthen your catapult by placing it in a warm oven for 10 minutes. If you wish, you could also coat the catapult with craft varnish once it has cooled—this will make it stronger.

1. Find a Y-shaped piece of wood when you're next in the woods. You may be lucky and find one on the ground; otherwise, ask an adult to help you use the penknife or garden cutters to chop a branch from a tree.

2. Use the penknife to cut the piece of wood down to the size you want—8in (20cm) is a good length to aim for if you're measuring from the tip of one of the Y-prongs to the end of the handle. Make sure the length of wood beneath the Y-prongs (the handle) is long enough for you to clasp your full palm around.

3. This step is optional, but fun. Carefully use the penknife (or potato peeler) to whittle away the bark from the wood. You could leave the bark on the handle and carve your initials into it.

4. Use the penknife or potato peeler to make a groove, 1in (2.5cm) from the tip, around each of the Y-prongs.

5. Position the two rubber bands in the grooves in the Y-frame. Use one hand to hold a fir cone firmly inside the other ends of the rubber bands, pull back, and fire.

17 Make a Conker Necklace

Thread some conkers onto a piece of string or shirring elastic to make a necklace or garland.

18 Make a Conker Hedgehog

Stick some shortened toothpicks (cocktail sticks) into the back of a conker to make a hedgehog. A conker in the corner of a room is said to keep spiders away. This is because it contains a natural, soap-like chemical compound called saponin. Perhaps you could try out this spider theory with your conker hedgehog. Others say that if a conker is split, it will keep moths at bay.

19 Make Conker Furniture

To make a stool or table, carefully push four pins (with colored heads if possible) into the non-shiny side of a conker to make the legs. If necessary, make small holes with a skewer or small precision screwdriver first.

To make a chair, push four colored pins into the underside of a conker (as for a stool). Push four or five more pins an equal distance apart, along one of the long upper sides of the conker. Weave 2¼in (6cm) strands of colored yarn in and out of the pin slats to make the chair back. Wind and knot each strand of yarn around the pins at the start and end of the chair back. (You may find it easier to pin the "chair back" pins into a pincushion while you weave and then transfer the back of the chair to the conker when it is finished.)

20 Play a Game of Conkers

The name "conker" may come from the word *conqueror* or originate from the word *conche* because the game was originally played with conch shells (snail shells). The first recorded game of conkers took place on the Isle of Wight, in England, in 1848. You need two players for a game of conkers.

What you need

- ★ Firm, unblemished conker
- ★ Skewer
- ★ Piece of string, 10in (25cm) in length
- ★ Small bowl (optional)
- ★ Vinegar or salt (optional)
- ★ Clear nail polish (optional)

1 Skewer a hole through the center of the conker. When you've made a hole all the way through, thread the conker onto the piece of string and tie a knot at the end. You're now ready to play conkers.

2 Traditionally, the first player is the person who is the first to say: "*Obli, obli, O, My first go.*"

3 Player One then holds the conker dangling from its string as still as possible.

4 Player Two—the striker—wraps his or her conker string around one hand and holds the conker in the other hand. He or she then releases the conker to strike Player One's conker. If Player Two misses, up to two further goes are allowed.

5 On striking the player traditionally says: "*Obli, obli, onker. My nut will conker.*"

6 If the strings get tangled, then the first player to shout "strings" gets an extra shot. If a player drops the conker, the other player can shout "stamps," and stamp on the conker. If, however, the owner shouts "stamps" first, then stamps is disallowed and the conker bashing continues.

7 Once Player Two has made a strike, Player One then takes turn as striker. The game continues until one of the conkers is so badly bashed that it can't be used. The conker that hasn't been destroyed is the winner.

TIPS

If you're playing this game in the wild, you don't need to prepare the conkers first. However, everyone wants a winning conker, so try strengthening the conker by soaking it in a bowl of vinegar or salt water overnight or painting it with clear nail polish. (You can also store conkers in a dark cupboard for a year.)

㉑ Make Leaf Bunting

This bunting project takes a while to complete, but you can break the instructions down into easy stages and do a little bit at a time. Leaves with the same shape have been used here, but you can vary the species and colors if you wish. The finished bunting makes a natural decoration.

What you need

★ Isosceles triangle or flag-shaped cardboard template, with two sides measuring 5–6in (12–15cm)

★ Enough newspaper for 15 pieces of bunting

★ Iron and ironing board

★ 3–4 pieces of wax (greaseproof) paper, measuring 8 x 8in (20 x 20cm), depending on the leaf size

★ 15 pressed leaves (see *Press Wild Flowers and Grasses*, on page 50)

★ Grater

★ Wax crayons

★ Glue

★ Long piece of string or nettle string (see *Make Nettle String*, on page 58), for hanging the bunting

★ Stapler

1 Use the cardboard template to cut a triangular shape from the bottom of the pieces of newspaper. You can create any shape you want, but make sure the top edge that you will attach to the string is straight.

2 Cover the center of the ironing board with some newspaper. Place one of the squares of wax (greaseproof) paper on top of the newspaper and put a pressed leaf in one half of the square.

3 Grate a few pieces of wax crayon over the leaf. Do not grate too much.

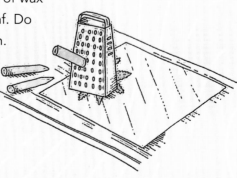

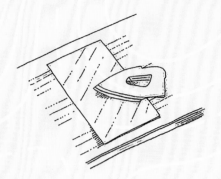

4 Fold the other half of the wax (greaseproof) paper over the leaf to cover it. Press a hot iron over the paper to melt the crayon—this should take no more than 5–6 seconds. The wax will stick to the leaf.

5 Repeat with a variety of colored crayons until all of the leaves have been colored. Replace the piece of wax (greaseproof) paper as necessary.

6 Glue a leaf (with the colored side facing outward) to the center of a piece of newspaper bunting. Leave enough paper at the top to make a 1in (2.5cm) fold for attaching the bunting to the string. Repeat until you have used all the leaves.

7 Fold the top of the first piece of bunting over the string and secure neatly at each end with the stapler. Leave enough space for sliding the bunting along the piece of string.

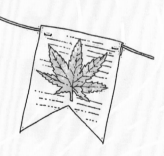

8 Attach the rest of the pieces of bunting in the same way, making sure you space them out evenly. Display your length of bunting outside or indoors.

Variation

You might like to make some bunting using leaf prints instead. Find as many differently shaped and sized leaves as you can and use newspaper or white or colored paper for the bunting. Protect your work surface with newspaper and have your paints ready. Paint the upper side of each leaf and then press this down firmly onto the bunting. Remove the leaf to reveal the leaf's print.

22 Climb a Tree

Get a different view of your woodland environment by climbing a tree. It's fun, challenging, and it will keep you fit! The closer the branches are, the easier it will be to climb the tree. Remember, take as much care getting down as you have going up.

23 Be a Woodland Detective

There are lots of things to look out for during a walk in the woods. Look closely and you'll be able to see which birds and animals inhabit the area. You may not be lucky enough to see some of the animals themselves, but you should be able to spot and study the clues they leave behind.

Look at tree trunk damage. It may have been nibbled by wildlife such as deer or rabbits that can't climb a tree, but what about mice—some of them can scamper up trees. Here are some more clues to help woodland detectives work out which creatures are in the woods:

- Upper trunk damage may be the work of a woodpecker or squirrel.
- Look for loose bark, where bats may roost.
- Look for a woodpecker's hole.
- Is the tree being used as a no-build roof for a burrowing animal? Perhaps for a fox, badger, rabbit, mouse, or vole?
- Look for heaps of cones—squirrels like to pile up cones to mark out their territory.
- Check out the size of the tunnel and compare this with the body widths of different animals.

- Look for mosses and lichens (abundant lichen growth is a sign of good air quality).
- Peeling bark may be the result of pollution or the bark's pores being blocked.

Find Out Who's Been Feasting!

If you're walking in a wood, look for nuts, fungi, and cones that have been nibbled by wildlife. With practice you'll be able to look at nibbled nuts, fungi, and cones, and work out which creatures have been feasting.

Cones

- Red and gray squirrels leave cones in open spaces with the scales eaten, leaving a clean-cut core.

- Mice are neat and tidy nibblers, and the cone will probably be hidden (i.e. not easy to find).

- Birds (e.g. woodpeckers) leave cones with ragged edges that are often jammed into holes in the bark of trees. There may be a pile of finished cones on the ground, beneath the cone that you've found in the bark.

Fungi

- Slugs make slimy dents.

- Birds leave pecked holes.

- Look for the incisor tooth marks left by deer.

- Mice leave small, gnawed marks.

Nuts

- A nut that has been coarsely cut in half is the work of a squirrel. Squirrels weigh nuts before opening them—they're smart. They don't waste their efforts on rotten or empty shells. Scientists have, however, played a trick on squirrels by filling two halves of a previously opened hazelnut with sand and then gluing them back together. They found that the squirrels weighed the sand-filled nuts before opening them. Rather a mean experiment, but you could try this out yourself if you find a stash of broken hazelnut shells and know where squirrels are in residence.

- A mouse holds a nut between its paws and turns it, as it chisels a rounded hole that is big enough to remove the kernel from the shell. It's a beautiful piece of craftsmanship that leaves a smooth, round rim. The hole is perfectly finished—a dormouse could be employed as a fairy clog-maker.

25 Spy on Woodland Bugs

The woods are full of insects to find and examine, so have a go at these bug-hunting activities.

- Turn over a small log and study the bugs that are living there. Be very quick and have your magnifying glass at the ready, because the bugs will scurry away from daylight.

- Hold a piece of white paper under a hanging branch and gently shake it. Look at the paper and see if any bugs have landed. Carefully put the paper on the ground and investigate further with your magnifying glass.

26 Spot these Woodland Creatures

Ssshhhh! If you're very quiet, you may be able to get a close view of some of this wonderful wildlife. You'll have to stay up late to see a bat awake, but these nocturnal creatures can be found hanging upside down from trees or caves in the daytime.

Mouse

Woodpecker

Fox

Bat

Vole

Rabbit

Stag

27 Make a Wild Flower Bouquet

Gather a range of common wild flowers for a pretty bouquet and give it to someone as a gift.

28 Make Potpourri

Collect some scented flower petals or herbs and dry them in a warm place such as an airing cupboard, on the back of a range cooker, or on top of a boiler. Use the petals and herbs as potpourri or pop them into a small fabric bag. Scented bags can be used to perfume a linen cupboard and drawers (see *Make Seaweed Bath Sacks*, on page 77 to find out how to make them). Sometimes potpourri becomes damp. If this happens, pop the basket or dish of potpourri somewhere warm until it is dry again.

29 Keep a Flower Diary

If you are interested in botany (the science of plants), then you might like to keep a diary of the wild flowers you spot when out exploring. Use your diary as a reference to look back on and share your findings with naturalist friends. Each year you'll be able to compare annual differences—for example, a cold spring will delay the appearance of flowers, while a warm spring will hasten this on. Here are a few useful tips to help you get started:

➡ Note where you see the flower.

➡ Draw the flower in bud, when open, and after it has seeded.

➡ Date each stage of the flower's development.

➡ Record the weather conditions.

➡ See if the flower's petals close on a dull day.

➡ Look for pollen on an anther—use some tape to remove a little and stick the pollen in your special diary.

➡ Take photographs of your finds and stick them in your diary.

➡ Add pressed flowers, grasses, and leaves to your diary (see page 50).

➡ Pop back at the same time the following year and write up your diary again—are the flowering and seeding dates the same?

30 Make a Flower Fairy

Tie a bunch of flowers to a stick and attach fern or fir wings. Name the fairy after the flowers you used.

31 Chant a False Oats Rhyme

There are various species of false oats grass, but any seeded grass will do for playing this rhyming game. Chant the rhyme: *"Here's a tree in summer, here's a tree in winter, here's a bunch of flowers, and here's an April shower"* as you perform the following actions:

1. Hold the grass—the tree in summer.

2. Run your finger and thumb up the grass to remove the seeds—the tree in winter.

3. Hold the seeds between your finger and thumb—the bunch of flowers.

4. Throw the seeds up in the air to fall on a friend—the April shower.

32 Make Miss Poppy

Y̶ou can make a flower fairy without even picking the flower. A common poppy flower is perfect for this, because the papery petals are flexible and the seedhead creates a perfect head. Carefully push the petals down to reveal the seedhead. Tie a blade of grass or piece of thread from your wild knapsack (see page 9) around the center of the fallen petals so that it looks like a belt. Poke a very thin, short corn stick (which is thinner than a toothpick/cocktail stick) through the petals above the belt of Miss Poppy's torso. The stick will act as the arms and, hey presto, you have a Miss Poppy. Miss Poppy will remain wild as she stands upright on her stalk and sways in the breeze.

33 Make a Fir Cone Family

W̶hile in the woods, you might like to craft some fir cones into people and animals (e.g. owls and penguins), or you can make fir-cone fairies to hang on Christmas trees. Acorns are also perfectly sized for crafting into Lilliputian people.

34 Whistle with a Blade of Grass

Different widths and thicknesses of grass will produce different whistle tones. Experiment with various grasses and reeds to see which makes the best whistle. Pick a wide and thick blade of grass, but remember never to pick grass near pets and animals (in case it's been in contact with animal waste).

(1) Lay the grass the length of the outside of one thumb.

(2) Slowly press the other thumb from the base of your hand up to make a small pocket between your thumbs with the blade of grass firmly in between. It needs to be taut (not slack), without any kinks in the grass.

(3) Purse your lips (by making a small hole in your mouth) and blow—you should hear a whistle.

(4) You can change the pitch of the whistle by moving or cupping your right hand to let air in and out. Be patient: if at first you don't succeed, try again. This is a reed instrument, not a whistle.

35 Make a Poppy Seed Necklace

Poppy seeds ripen in a dry fruit capsule. This fruit is perfect for threading onto a length of colored shirring elastic to make a pretty wild necklace. Nature has given the poppy fruit or pistil (the female part of the flower) a very interesting shape and its top is colored with a glint of gold—no paint spray is required. In the wild, if the poppy fruit is left to grow, the seeds float away in the breeze from tiny holes at the top of the seedhead.

Press Wild Flowers and Grasses

What you need

★ Lots of heavy books

★ 2 x letter size (A4) sheets of blotting paper

★ Selection of wild flowers, leaves, pretty herbs, or grasses (freshly picked for good color retention and as dry as possible)

★ Pair of tweezers

★ Glue (optional)

Dried and pressed flowers and grasses can be used in craft projects or to build up a herbarium (a collection of preserved plants). A flower press can be useful for pressing flowers and grasses, but heavy books and blotting paper work just as well. Remember only to pick and press common flowers from areas where there are lots of flowers growing and not protected flowers such as cowslips.

1 Open a big book and lay a sheet of blotting paper on one page.

2 Carefully place the flowers, leaves, herbs, or grasses on the blotting paper, so that they are flat, but not touching each other.

3 Use the tweezers to position the petals and leaves so that they will flatten evenly.

4 Gently place the second sheet of blotting paper on top of the specimens and close the book.

5 Put the book in a place where it won't be disturbed and rest heavy books on top. Forget about the flowers for at least three weeks and, if you can, wait four weeks before you take a peep.

6 Remove the books and lift out the pressed flowers, leaves, herbs, or grasses.

7 Glue your pressed flowers, leaves, herbs, or grasses to greetings cards, postcards, or pictures.

37 Make a Daisy Chain

Find a daisy patch and pick some daisies. Use your thumb to make a small slit in the stem of a daisy. Slip the stalk of another daisy through the slit and gently pull the second daisy through. Repeat with another daisy until you have created a chain. Finish the circle by making a second slit in the daisy you started with and pulling through the last daisy stem. You can also try this idea with clover or other soft-stemmed flowers.

38 Make Flower Jewelry

You can use the purple flowers of creeping thistle to make a bracelet or necklace. Use scissors to cut at least 20 creeping thistle flower heads (you'll need more for a necklace). When you get home, remove any spiky thorns from the flower heads with tweezers. Use a needle with a large eye and some green tapestry thread or yarn to sew through the black base of each flower head to make a chain. Tie the ends of the threads together and you have pretty bracelet or necklace.

You may prefer to use a meadowland flower called knapweed instead. This also has purple flowers but, unlike creeping thistle, it doesn't have spiky thorns. Another idea for making a bracelet is to wrap some sticky tape, with the sticky side facing out, around your wrist and be creative on a walk: stop, pick, and stick flowers to your wild bracelet.

39 Make a Honeysuckle Crown

Cut a length of honeysuckle that will fit around your head, loop it, and then secure the circle with some string, if you need to. Often a double honeysuckle circle can be twisted to make a crown without the need for string. Pop other flowers into the circle if you wish. If you want to keep biting insects away, then add some sweet gale or bog myrtle. You can also dry sweet gale and use it to scent drawers.

40 Make a Teasel Wizard

Teasels grow in damp ground and can become very tall. The spiky flower heads of teasels were used by the textile industry to comb or "tease" out the fibers in fabrics. The Romans called the teasel *Lavacrum veneris*—basin of Venus—because the leaves are joined at the base and fill with water after rain, like a cup. Indeed, if you look closely into the leaves of teasel after a shower of heavy rain, you may see tiny insects that have drowned in a teasel swimming pool. Bees and butterflies visit teasels for nectar and its thousands of seeds are enjoyed by birds.

If you cut off the thorns and are wary of the purple, conical, and prickly flower head, teasels make brilliant stick people. Little else is required because the flower becomes the head, the central stalk acts as the body, and the leaves look like a frilly petticoat.

41 Make a Wild Bling Bracelet

You can thread different seeds onto a short length of shirring elastic to make a wild bling bracelet. Older children can use a skewer to make a hole through the middle of some acorns or small conkers, and thread these onto the elastic. Alternatively, simply tie the elastic around some little alder cones.

42 Spot these Common Plants

Look out for these plants in hedgerows and meadows. With permission, you could change the mowing pattern of your garden lawn and start your own mini wild meadow.

Buttercups

Scabious

Violets

Chickweed

Blackberries

Sheep sorrel

Hedgerow garlic

43 Watch a Plant Set Seed

Spring is the start of the growing season, which for a plant begins with a seed. This is a good time for young naturalists to choose a plant and follow its life cycle as the seasons pass. Find a germinated seedling, visit the spot regularly with a notepad and pencil, and keep a record of how the seedling develops into a new plant before producing seed of its own.

44 Tell the Time with a Dandelion Clock

First find your seeded dandelion and then blow. Count the puffs—counting an hour for each puff and blow until all the seed has blown away. Dandelion clocks tell different times to different children. Some children will blow hard, others will blow gently, and what of the wind? Sometimes it helps with time-keeping too. When you blow on a dandelion clock, you're helping nature by spreading the seeds. In spring, try adding young dandelion leaves to salads.

45 Make Rosehip Itching Powder

In France rosehips are called *gratte-cul* or "scratch your arse," which is rather rude. Scottish children call rosehips Itchy Coos. Beware of playing this trick on friends with allergies or sensitive skins.

Collect some ripe rosehips, snapping off the leaves and prickly stalks as you pick. Wear some gardening gloves to do this. Wash the hips and then put them

onto a tray lined with paper. Dry the berries in a warm, airy place for two weeks until they are wrinkly and hard. You can also dry the hips in a low oven or food dehydrator if you wish. Cut open the shriveled berries and take out the fine hairs—these are your itching powder. You can keep the leftover seeds for wild cooking or feed them to the birds. Store your itching powder in an airtight jar or envelope. Then, let the itching begin—sprinkle some itching powder down the back of a friend's neck.

You can also make itching powder from whirlygigs or maple seeds. Gently rub two maple seeds together over a sheet of paper and tiny hairs will fall onto the paper. Store this itching powder in a small pot or envelope.

46 Make Nettle String

The stems of stinging nettles are very tough and strong, which makes them ideal for making wild string or cordage. Nettles can be found nearly everywhere, especially in wastelands and other neglected places. Remember to wear gloves when handling stinging nettles. Pop your finished nettle string in your wild knapsack, as you never know when it will prove useful.

What you need

★ Pair of gardening gloves

★ Scissors

★ 3–4 stinging nettles

★ Small stone

★ Bowl of water

★ Sturdy twig (for storing the nettle)

1 Put on the gloves and cut some nettles with the scissors. (If you are in the garden, and have asked your parents' permission first, pull the nettles up by the roots.)

2 Rub the nettles up and down with your gloved hands to remove the leaves and tiny hairs from the stems.

3 Lay the first nettle stem on a garden table or on the ground, and use the stone to flatten the stalk. The best place to bash the stalk is on its knobbly nodes.

4 Remove the woody, yellow center from the stem and throw this away. Repeat this process for the other nettle stems.

5 Keep the outer fibers and leave them to dry in the sun or indoors. The nettle fibers will shrink as they dry.

6 Soak the dry nettle strands in a bowl of water until they're damp. Take two of the strands and lay them out flat. Find a friend and give them one end of the two strands, while you take the other end. You both need to twiddle the strands in opposite directions between your index finger and thumb to create a single piece of string.

7 Decide at the start which person is going to twiddle to the left and which person to the right. You can add to the thickness of the piece of string by twiddling more strands of nettle together.

8 Tie a knot in both ends of the nettle string and wrap it around the twig until needed.

47 Make a Wild Bird Garland

This simple garland is easily adapted to suit the season and you can use whatever is in the store cupboard. Some people like to thread popcorn and dried fruits on a garland to decorate their Christmas tree—you can do this with wild edibles too. The birds will appreciate your hard work as they snack on the garland on a cold day after Christmas. For a free and really wild garland, get outside and forage seeds and berries, instead of raiding the kitchen store cupboard. If you have a fir tree in the garden, this is perfect for draping a garland over, but a bush will do just as well. The birds aren't fussy. You can make your garland as short or long as you like, although the longer the garland, the greater the number of wild edibles you'll need to forage.

What you need

★ 78in (200cm) strong embroidery floss (thread) or 39in (100cm) thin craft string or nettle string (see Make Nettle String, on page 58)

★ Tapestry needle (with a large eye)

★ Collection of small bowls

★ Selection of wild haws, hips, seeds, thistledown, and small cones (such as alder cones)

★ Ready-to-eat popcorn (air- not oil-popped, so it is not greasy)

★ Dried fruit

★ Fresh cranberries, blueberries, and blackberries (as in season and not over-ripe)

1 Thread the embroidery floss or string through the tapestry needle. If you are using embroidery floss, then double up the thread. (If you are using thicker string or nettle string, use the tapestry needle or a small screwdriver to make a hole very carefully in the berry etc., and thread without using a needle.)

2 Put each of the ingredients in a separate bowl to make it easier to choose what to thread onto your garland next.

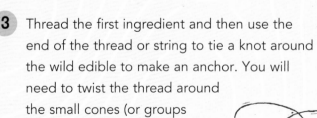

3 Thread the first ingredient and then use the end of the thread or string to tie a knot around the wild edible to make an anchor. You will need to twist the thread around the small cones (or groups of cones).

4 Continue threading the wild and store-cupboard ingredients onto the embroidery floss or string. Try to create a colorful pattern as you thread. Make sure you don't use anything too soft and squishy or too thick (e.g. nuts), which can make the task tricky and messy.

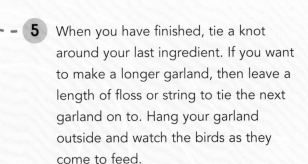

5 When you have finished, tie a knot around your last ingredient. If you want to make a longer garland, then leave a length of floss or string to tie the next garland on to. Hang your garland outside and watch the birds as they come to feed.

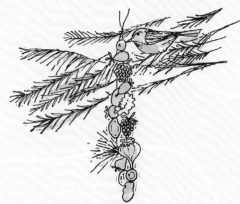

TIP
Lay the berries and hips you have collected on an open tray and put this in the freezer. Pack the frozen edibles in plastic bags and label them clearly: *For the Birds.* You can use the berries throughout the year.

48 Make Huck Finn's Wild Ink

You can easily use mud for war paint, but any wild edible berry that stains is tastier. You'll probably have a good idea of which berries to use from foraging—just look at your hands. Choose berries that are ripe. Bilberries—known as huckleberries in the USA—produce a purple/red ink but actually write in blue, while raspberries are great for writing in pink.

1. Put 3 level tablespoons of bilberries or raspberries and 1 teaspoon of water in a small saucepan. Cover the pan with a lid and cook the berries over a low heat for 5–7 minutes until they collapse. You may need to add a little more water to stop the berries sticking to the pan. Leave the berries to cool.

2. Push the berries through a small plastic sieve into a small glass jar. You will now have very thick ink. You can add a few drops of seawater or salted tap water if the ink is too thick (when cooled), but don't add too much.

3. Store the ink in the refrigerator. The ink won't last very long, so... grab some paper, dip your writing utensil into your natural ink, and start writing or drawing—you won't find a bottle of this in stores.

TIP
You could use bivalve shells collected from the beach as wild ink containers.

49 Blackberry-Dye a Handkerchief

Dyed handkerchiefs can make original gifts for family and friends, so try this idea.

What you need

- ★ ¾ cup (100g) blackberries from a hedgerow (shaken to remove any insects)

- ★ ⅓ cup (100ml) rainwater

- ★ Saucepan

- ★ Potato masher

- ★ Sieve

- ★ Bowl

- ★ *For the mordant to fix the color:* ⅓ cup (100ml) water and 1 teaspoon (5g) salt

- ★ Spoon

- ★ Shallow dish

- ★ Small handkerchief

1 Put the blackberries and rainwater in the saucepan and cook over a low heat for about 5–10 minutes until the blackberries have collapsed. Gently bash the blackberries with the potato masher and then leave the mixture to cool.

2 Strain the blackberry juice through the sieve into the bowl.

3 To make the mordant, use the spoon to stir and dissolve the salt in the water (make sure you use enough water to cover the handkerchief) in the shallow dish.

4 Soak the handkerchief in the salt water for approximately 20 minutes.

5 Squeeze out as much liquid as you can and pop the handkerchief into the blackberry dye.

6 Leave the handkerchief soaking in the dye for as long as you want. Leave overnight if you want to produce a bright red handkerchief.

7 Wring the dye from the handkerchief and hang out to dry on a washing line.

50 Rose-Dye a Handkerchief

Dyeing a handkerchief is a good place to start, so have a go at this fun project.

What you need

★ 1¾oz (50g) *Rosa rugosa* petals from a hedgerow (shaken to remove any insects)

★ Saucepan

★ Rainwater

★ Potato masher

★ Sieve

★ Bowl

★ *For the mordant to fix the color:* ¼ cup (50ml) vinegar and ¾ cup (200ml) water

★ Spoon

★ Shallow dish

★ Small handkerchief

1. Put the petals in a saucepan and cover with rainwater. Put the pan on the stovetop and bring to the boil (lots of bubbles). Lower the heat to a simmer (small bubbles) and cook for about 2 hours until the petals are white, not pink. Gently bash the petals with the potato masher and leave to cool.

2. Strain the pink rose water through the sieve into the bowl. Squeeze the petals to remove all of the water.

3. To make the mordant, mix the vinegar and water in the shallow dish and soak the handkerchief for 30 minutes. Squeeze out as much of the liquid as you can and then pop the handkerchief into the rose dye.

4. Leave the handkerchief soaking in the dye for as long as you want. Leave overnight for a bright pink handkerchief, less time for a paler pink.

5. Wring the dye from the handkerchief and hang out to dry on a washing line.

NOTE: When dyeing pieces of fabric with most plants and berries, you'll need to use a mordant such as vinegar or salt to fix the color of the dye. Vinegar is used to fix plant dyes and salt is used to fix berry dyes.

51 Turn Bluebells Pink

Acid can alter wild ink colors. In spring, find an ant nest and put a slightly squished Spanish bluebell on top. The ants will investigate and spray a jet of formic acid on the bluebell. Wait and see what happens—the bluebell will turn into a pinkbell. This change is due to the flower's blue pigment anthocyanin being exposed to acid. You could also try this experiment with garden lobelia.

52 Keep a Wild Color Diary

Keeping a wild color diary will help you to learn about natural dyes. The weather, season, and location, as well as the type of water and cooking pot—large, stainless-steel pots are best—will all affect the color of the dye. Write notes on:

★ The weather, place, and date that you picked the plant or berry.

★ The fabric you used—natural fabrics such as silk, cotton, and wool work best.

★ How much of the plant or berry, as well as water, you used.

★ How long you cooked/left the material in the dye.

★ How much mordant you used.

★ Stick a color swatch (tester strip) of your dyed fabrics in your diary.

53 Spot these Insects

Explore your outdoor environment very carefully and you may be lucky enough to find these insects. Be careful not to disturb the buzzy bee or he may greet you with a sting!

Ladybugs

Bees

Grasshoppers

Moths

Ants

Butterflies

54 Build an Insect Hotel

You can build a hotel for insects in any secret, well-camouflaged place by gathering and piling high plenty of branches and twigs. Visit regularly—just like a hotel inspector—and bear in mind that some of your detective work may well be underground. Take a magnifying glass, and your pocket I.D. book, notebook, and pencil.

55 Investigate Ants

Spend some time watching these fascinating and busy little creatures.

What you need

★ Teaspoon

★ 4 live ants

★ Clean glass jar with a lid

★ Small screwdriver (for putting holes in the lid)

★ Moist greenery (such as dandelion or chickweed leaves)

★ Sugar

★ Magnifying glass

1 Use a teaspoon to collect 4 live ants (from the same area and hopefully the same colony) and pop them in the glass jar. Put on the lid. Make sure you have put holes in the lid using the screwdriver to provide ventilation.

2 Tilt the jar, add some greenery, and put a pinch of sugar down one side of the jar. Replace the lid and leave the jar on its side. What do the ants do?

3 Using the magnifying glass, observe the ants and ask yourself questions such as: Do the ants use their feelers to touch each other? How do the ants behave as individuals and as a group?

4 Visit your glass jar after dark to see what happens when you turn on a light. Do ants rest?

5 Release the ants when you have jotted down your observations.

56 Have an Ant Dinner Party

This is a fun dinner party with a difference! The best part is you can eat any leftover candy afterward!

What you need

Ant Menu One

★ Cake or cookie (biscuit) crumbs

★ Sugar

★ Small cubes of carrot

★ Shredded dandelion leaf

Ant Menu Two

★ Selection of candies (such as jelly beans) with grape, apple, strawberry, orange, blackcurrant, lime, and lemon flavors

Ant Menu Three

★ Red, orange, blue, green, yellow, pink, violet, and brown colored candies (of the same variety)

1. Scatter the food from *Menu One* in piles in an area where there is ant activity.

2. Wait patiently and see what the ants choose to eat.

3. Place the colored candies from *Menu Two* in a different area and again wait for the ants to choose their food. The candies are flavored—does this seem to influence the ants' food choice?

4. Repeat Step 3 for *Menu Three*. The results of this experiment will tell you whether ants have a color preference in the foods they eat.

Spot these at the Beach

Enhance your walk along the beach by trying to find some of these superb marine plants and sea creatures.

Seaweeds

Starfish

Periwinkles

Crabs

Limpets

Mussels

Spot these Seaweeds

When you are walking along the beach or having fun in the waves, see how many types of seaweed you can spot. Different seaweeds flourish in different areas of the seashore.

Carrageen

Dead man's rope

Dulse

Kelp

59 Collect Seaweed

There are a few rules to bear in mind when collecting seaweed from the seashore for use at home:

★ DON'T pick storm-cast seaweed for cooking; only use seaweed that is growing.

★ DO use a pair of scissors to cut seaweeds from their holdfasts at low tide on a clean beach. (Remember to take scissors with you when you visit the beach.)

★ DON'T cook with floating seaweed or seaweed that grows at the top of the shore near drains. Sea lettuce and sea grass like growing here—instead, pick these seaweeds from rock pools at low tide.

★ DO wash the seaweed in the sea so that any hidden "visitors" can find a new home locally. You should also rinse the seaweed in some cold water when you get home.

★ DO use a separate bag for each type collected, as this will make it easier to sort out your seaweeds when you get home.

60 Dry and Store Seaweed

When you get home, wash the seaweed thoroughly. Rinse it in cold water and squeeze out as much of the water as possible. A salad spinner is helpful here—spin the seaweed around, just as you would if preparing salad leaves. Next dry the seaweed. Lay the pieces of seaweed on a tray lined with newspaper or some paper towel—making sure that they aren't touching—and leave to dry on a sunny windowsill. You could also pop the tray in a warm airing cupboard. On a sunny day, you can dry larger seaweeds such as sugar kelp by pegging them on a washing line. You can also dry seaweed on trays in a low oven or even in a food dehydrator if you have one. Some people dry seaweed in a hot oven, but you *must* be eagle-eyed if you do this and make sure that the seaweed does not burn.

When you have dried the seaweed, cut it into manageable lengths or grind it in a food-blender. It is easier to grind a little at a time, pop it in an airtight container, and then repeat the process until you have used up all of the seaweed. Shake the containers when you remember and use the dried seaweed as a flavoring, just as you would herbs or spices.

61 Mount Light Seaweed

Lightweight seaweeds can be mounted to make pretty greetings cards or for a seaweed library. You may like to put the mounted seaweeds into poly-pocket files or in a scrapbook, as 19th-century children did. The first mounting may be a little tricky but, like learning to ride a bicycle, it becomes easier with practice.

What you need

★ Scissors

★ Selection of light seaweeds

★ Small bowl of cold water

★ Small paintbrush

★ Piece of thick card or paper, measuring 6 x 6in (15 x 15cm)

★ Tweezers or a toothpick

★ Pile of heavy books

1. Use scissors to cut some seaweed at low tide.

2. When you return home, rinse the seaweed and put it in a bowl of cold water to keep cool. Never leave it in a hot place. (If you're busy, you can keep the seaweed in the refrigerator for a day.)

3. Take the seaweed you want to press and use the paintbrush to brush it dry. Use scissors to trim the specimen to fit your piece of card or paper. You can use a larger piece of letter size (A4) card and more fronds if you would like to poly-pocket file your seaweed.

4. Place the seaweed on the piece of card or paper, and use a wet paintbrush to gently position the seaweed. Then use the tweezers or toothpick to arrange the seaweed.

5. Leave the card or paper on a sunny windowsill to dry. Seaweeds contain a sticky substance and so should stick without glue. When the seaweed looks dry, carefully put some heavy books on top of the card or paper and leave for a further 2–3 weeks.

6. Label the card or paper with the seaweed's species, as well as the date and place you picked it.

62 Make Seaweed Bath Sacks

These easy-to-make bags make a lovely seaside vacation memory or gift. Younger children can practice knots as they tie the sacks. Soak the bath sack in your bath water for 5 minutes before you use it, unless, of course, you want to spend a long time in the bath. As the seaweed rehydrates, it releases a gel that has skin-softening properties.

What you need

★ Dried seaweed, cut or broken by hand into short lengths

★ Jelly bag, pop sock, or a leg of pantyhose (tights), cut below the knee

★ Ribbon, for tying (optional)

1 Stuff the dried seaweed into the jelly bag, pop sock, or section of pantyhose.

2 Tie a knot (and a ribbon, if using) tightly at the top to make a sack. You can use colored or patterned pop socks or pantyhose if you wish to make your bath sacks look really pretty.

63 Make Wild Rose and Carrageen Soap

What you need

- ★ 2 teaspoons (10g) dried carrageen (see page 75 to find out how to dry seaweed)
- ★ Bowl
- ★ Saucepan
- ★ 1oz (25g) *Rosa rugosa* petals
- ★ Potato masher
- ★ Spoon
- ★ Sieve
- ★ 5–6 drops red food coloring (optional)
- ★ Small glass jar or plastic container with a secure lid

Making your own soap is great fun and means you can be sure it only contains natural ingredients. Seaweed can be used in lots of bathing and beauty products. You will enjoy washing up the utensils used to make this soap because the gel from the carrageen feels lovely and soft. This recipe makes one small jar or container.

1 Put the dried carrageen in a bowl and cover with water for about 10 minutes. When the carrageen has soaked up the water, squeeze it well to remove excess water and pop it in a saucepan.

2 Add the rose petals to the pan and just enough water to cover. Cook over a low heat and simmer for about 30 minutes until the mixture is very, very thick. Mash the mixture with a potato masher every so often to make sure that it doesn't stick to the pan. Remove the pan from the heat and leave to cool for 5 minutes.

3 Spoon the mixture into a sieve over a bowl and use the spoon to push as much of the cold rose and carrageen soap through the sieve as possible. Remove the sieve and stir in the red food coloring if you wish.

4 Put the soap in a small glass jar or plastic container, put on the lid, and store in the refrigerator between bath times. Use the soap within 7 to 10 days.

64 Make Cucumber and Carrageen Soap

You can also make soap using carrageen and grated cucumber. Follow the recipe and instructions for the *Wild Rose and Carrageen Soap* (see opposite), but use ½ small cucumber (instead of the *Rosa rugosa* petals) and 4–5 drops of green food coloring (optional). Before adding the cucumber to the pan of carrageen, first grate it into a bowl using the coarse (big) blade of a grater— stop before you reach the end of the cucumber or you may cut yourself. You can also add a handful of wild mint leaves to the mixture to give your soap a mint fragrance. Put the finished soap in a small glass jar or plastic container with a secure lid and store in a refrigerator. Use your soap within 7 to 10 days.

65 Spot Arthropods and Mollusks

Explore your coastal surroundings to discover some of these incredible creatures. Tread carefully as you go!

Limpets
MOLLUSK
GASTROPOD

Cockles
MOLLUSK
BIVALVE

Oysters
MOLLUSK
BIVALVE

Crabs
ARTHROPOD

Whelks
MOLLUSK
GASTROPOD

Mussels
MOLLUSK
BIVALVE

BARNACLES
ARTHROPOD

Octopus
MOLLUSK
CEPHALOPOD

Scallops
MOLLUSK
BIVALVE

Squid
MOLLUSK
CEPHALOPOD

66 Be a Shell-Seeker

At the beach it's fun to paddle in the shallow waters and look for colorful pebbles and shells, or perhaps some shellfish for supper. Take your fishing net so that you can examine the sea life that thrives in the rock pools—seize your moment because the tide will return and your rock pool will disappear. You'll see more colors and details if you rinse the shells in seawater to make them wet. Take a net to the beach so that you can study different shells in the shallow waters. Common shells for shell-seekers include the common whelk and common periwinkle. Common periwinkles are easy to prise from the rocks, but their rounded shape is clever, protecting them from big waves.

67 Look for Limpets

Limpets are very common on rocks and stones. They have a very strong foot, which they use to stick to the rocks. It is said that you have one go at knocking a limpet from its rock and, if you don't succeed, it will be impossible the second time. This is where the expression "to stick like a limpet" comes from. Older boys and girls may try to disprove this theory, but I suggest: one go and, if you miss, leave the limpet alone. The limpet shell protects the limpet as it presses against the rock; it looks like an Asian conical hat. The waves wash over the limpet's shell, but their force cannot move it from the rock. If you succeed in removing the limpet, then examine the muscular foot that the limpet uses to move around as it grazes on seaweed.

68 Craft with Shells

Wash your shells to remove any sand, pat them dry with some paper towel, and then place the shells on some newspaper on a windowsill to dry. Coat the shells with clear varnish if you want to make them sparkle. You can use shells to decorate greetings cards, matchboxes, jewelry boxes, and pen pots or tie a few shells together to make a tree decoration. Or you can also try making pieces of jewelry with them. For example, you could wrap some colorful craft cord around a pretty shell and then tie the cord securely to make a simple necklace or bracelet—this is something you could do while still at the beach. If you are lucky enough to find any small shells with predator-bored holes, you can thread seaweed, such as bootlace or dead man's rope, craft cord, or shirring elastic through the hole, and then secure the ends to make a necklace.

69 Explore Rock Pools

When the tide goes out, seawater sometimes becomes trapped in rocks until the tide comes in again. On a sunny day the water in rock pools can become very warm—rock pools are nature's paddling pools. They are exciting places to explore with a fishing net, but make sure that you return sea animals to the pool after you have had a good look at them. Seaweeds cover some rocks but, if you peep underneath, you may find periwinkles, limpets, and whelks hiding. Snails eat seaweed but larger creatures crawl about in rock pools too. Crabs eat snails and, although you won't see the food chain in action, you may see a crab scuttle away if you lift up a small rock. Plant-eating animals are called herbivores. Herbivores are eaten by meat-eaters (e.g. the crab) and these animals are called carnivores. On a hot day rock-pool residents are exposed to the sun but, fortunately, nature is kind and each animal adapts to the heat in its own way. The returning seawater will cover up the rock pool and refresh the sea life, but you'll have to await the next low tide to continue your exploring adventures. The tide waits for no man.

70 Spot these Sand Creatures

Sand is home to some wonderful creatures. Take a look for these on your explorations.

Goose barnacles For a long time, barnacles were classified as mollusks because of their shell, but 19th-century scientists decided that they are, in fact, crustaceans. Barnacles are loosely grouped as goose barnacles and acorn barnacles. Goose barnacles are sometimes called gooseneck barnacles because they use a stalk to attach themselves permanently to driftwood or shipwrecks. They are rather strange-looking, but Charles Darwin thought that barnacles were very interesting and spent eight years studying them. This work helped him develop his theory of evolution.

Beach hoppers are easy to identify because they hop. You can often spy them burrowed under seaweed trying to keep cool. Beach hoppers are crustaceans and look like a flattened shrimp. They are sometimes unkindly called sand fleas, but they won't hurt you.

Blood worms leave tiny holes in the sand, which you can see at low tide. They burrow into the sand but only go down so far because there is not enough oxygen in wet sand for them to live.

Sanderlings are small, pale gray wading birds with long legs that live on sandy beaches. I call them groupies because they meet up and rush about energetically at the point where the sea breaks on to the sand. When one flies off, the rest quickly follow.

71 Skip with Seaweed

A length of seaweed can double up as an excellent skipping rope—look out for a thin seaweed called bootlace, mermaid tresses, or dead man's rope. This seaweed lends itself to skipping games. You may find one lengthy enough for long rope games.

72 Make a Mollusk Wind Chime

A wind chime made from attractive mollusk shells will remind you of the seashore as it dances noisily in the breeze. When you visit the beach, search for shells that have a natural hole. Empty limpet shells, for example, may already have a neat, circular hole in the middle—made by the limpet's predator—which means you can just thread the craft cord through the hole. Bivalve twin mollusks, such as mussels, cockles, and razor clams, are useful if the two halves of the shell are still attached to each other, because the cord for hanging each shell can be twisted and secured at the shell's natural hinge. This means that you don't have to tie a knot—how shell-crafty is this? (Some coastal areas are treeless, which is why a clothes hanger has been used here, but you could also attach the shells to a stick and suspend your chime with some string.)

What you need

★ 12 empty mollusk shells (such as limpets and bivalve mussels, cockles, or razor clams)

★ Bowl of warm, soapy water

★ Spray craft varnish (optional)

★ 12 lengths of colored craft cord, 10–12in (25–30cm) in length

★ Colored plastic clothes hanger

★ Large piece of dulse (optional)

1 Wash your selection of mollusk shells in a bowl of warm, soapy water and dry them carefully.

2 Spray the shells with craft varnish if you want glitzy shells, and leave to dry.

3 Attach each shell to a length of craft cord by threading the cord though the natural hole and tying a knot at one end. You can also just tie the cord around the shell, but this won't be as secure. If you're lucky enough to have joined bivalve shells, simply twist the cord around the hinge.

4 Arrange the threaded shells attractively and then tie the other end of each cord securely around the lower bar of the clothes hanger. Make sure you space the cords so the shells will bounce into each other in the breeze. Attach a large piece of dulse for added color if you wish. The color of the seaweed will fade over time.

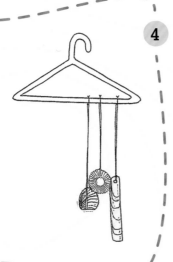

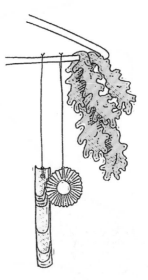

5 Hang the finished wind chime in front of an open window or perhaps in the garden.

Variation
Seaweed and Shell Wind Chime

When you're at the beach, look for a pretty shell attached to a piece of seaweed (often a member of the wrack family), because this will be perfect for your chime. Simply tie some craft cord to the top of the dried seaweed and then shorten the cord to keep the dangling shells to the same length.

73 Play Beach Hopscotch

Hopscotch is a fun hopping game that you can easily play at the beach. Try to finish your game before the tide comes in again and washes away the grid in the sand. The rules are: you can only put one foot in each square; you have to hop over the square onto which the marker pebble has been thrown; you have to balance on one foot when the pebble has been thrown onto one of the double squares—this is the difficult bit.

What you need

★ A sandy beach

★ Seaweeds, shells, and flotsam, for naming the grid squares (optional)

★ A marker pebble

(1) Draw a hopscotch grid in the sand, as shown here. You can make a longer or shorter grid, if you wish. The design doesn't really matter, but each square needs to be large enough for you to fit one foot in.

(2) Use the seaweeds, shells, and flotsam that you've collected to name each square. If you are in a hurry, then just use a pebble to mark traditional numbers in the squares.

(3) The idea of the game is to hop on one foot in a single square and with both feet in a double square. The first player throws a marker pebble into the first square and then hops over this square and through the hopscotch grid. If the player gets through, they turn round and hop back through the grid to the start. The player then throws their pebble into the second square, and so on. If the player lands on a line or tumbles out of the grid, their turn ends.

74 Create Beach Art

Collect some shells, pebbles, kelp stipes, and flotsam, and arrange them in shapes (e.g. a heart, star, or flower) or perhaps shape the shells and pebbles into a message. Use your imagination in your art and beach games. You can build sculptures by carefully piling things on top of each other. If you have some string in your knapsack, you can use this to make your creation stable. Sadly, more and more trash is being washed up on beaches, but you can put jetsam to good use in your beach art. Make sure that you take trash home with you when you have finished your beach art and dispose of it properly. We need to keep our beaches clean and tidy—like our bedrooms.

75 Go Pond Dipping

Morning and early afternoon are the best times for pond dipping because small creatures respond to the sun's warmth and there is plenty of light for you to study them. Most wildlife lives among the plants at the edges of rivers and ponds, rather than in open water, so this is the best (and easiest) place to start dipping. The equipment you'll need is inexpensive, but you might like to make your own pond dipping net (see page 96). Opposite are some helpful tips for pond dipping:

76 Be a Pollution Detective

Collect water from a pond or river in a jar and become a pollution detective. The presence or absence of plant and animal life can act as a guide to levels of pollution.

➡ If the water is clean you may see mayflies and stoneflies. They're the first to buzz off if water is polluted. Trout and minnow only live in clean water too. The diversity of plants and invertebrates is also a clue to the overall health of the water.

➡ Natural waste from living and dead freshwater organisms is "recycled" by tiny organisms called bacteria—it's humans who cause pollution. If you see dumped trash in a pond or river, tell your local environmental agency and offer to help with organized pond and river conservation.

★ Vary your dipping area, if you can. Remember that plants and animals differ according to habitat. Some are found in deep water, others near the surface.

★ Tread slowly and quietly as you near the water so that your reflection and vibrations from your footsteps do not frighten away tadpoles, beetles, and small fish from the shallow water. Think like a predator.

★ Take jars, lids with air holes, and white food trays with you for collecting bugs. Plastic bottles and buckets are especially useful because they won't break. (A large plastic bottle with the narrow top cut off makes a cheap bucket.)

★ A kitchen sieve is helpful for looking through fine gravel and mud. You'll find a pair of tweezers, a white plastic spoon, and a small paintbrush useful too, so remember to pop these in your wild knapsack (see page 8). A white (to help visibility) ic-cube tray also has lots of compartments for viewing tiny bugs.

★ Keep a pocket magnifying glass, notebook, and pencil close at hand.

★ Sweep your net quickly in a figure-of-eight pattern and tip the contents into your jar, tray, or bucket as soon as you can.

★ Look among the leaves and twigs at the bottom of the pond with your dipping net.

★ Sift through water plants and grasses trailing in water. Use your paintbrush or white plastic spoon to gently flick insects into jars.

★ In fast-flowing streams, look under large stones or on the bank sides.

★ Transfer the bugs to a jar or white food tray half-filled with pond water. The white background of the tray will make it easier to study the bugs with a magnifying glass.

★ Jot down plants and animals as you spot them in your notepad, because your memory is never as good as the wild experience. Keep a dated pond diary if you visit regularly.

★ Pond wildlife is small and delicate, and can be easily harmed. All creatures and plant material should be returned to the pond once you've looked at them.

77 Make Artist's Charcoal

If you are a budding naturalist artist, you might like to try using willow twigs to produce charcoal. Charcoal is easy to make—you've probably seen charcoaled sticks in the embers of a bonfire. Try to avoid using young or treated wood. This is because young wood produces soft, powdery charcoal and treated wood may give off toxic fumes. Also shun very thin twigs because the wood will shrink as it turns to charcoal and the charcoal will be too thin to draw with. You'll need to make sure that the twigs you use are dry too. Harder woods take longer to turn to charcoal, with the exact charring time depending on the thickness of the sticks and the number of twigs wrapped in the package, so have lots of fun experimenting. As with everything, practice makes perfect.

What you need

★ Penknife

★ 6 twigs of dry, soft wood (such as willow or pine), 6in (15cm) in length and no thicker than your thumb

★ 5 squares of kitchen foil, 14 x 14in (35 x 35cm)

★ Barbecue

★ Pair of tongs

1. Use the penknife to remove any joints in the twigs so that they are as straight as possible. This will make it easier to hold them.

2. Carefully scrape the bark from the twigs with the penknife.

3. Lay the twigs on a square of foil and wrap this tightly around them to make a parcel. Make sure there isn't any air in the package, because air will encourage ash and not charcoal. Continue to wrap with the remaining sheets of foil.

4. Place the package on the grid of a barbecue and when the flames have died down—or once you've finished cooking your sausages—use a pair of tongs to push the package into the center of the hot coals. Pile the coals around the package and leave overnight.

5. In the morning, when the package is completely cold, unwrap your charcoal and start drawing.

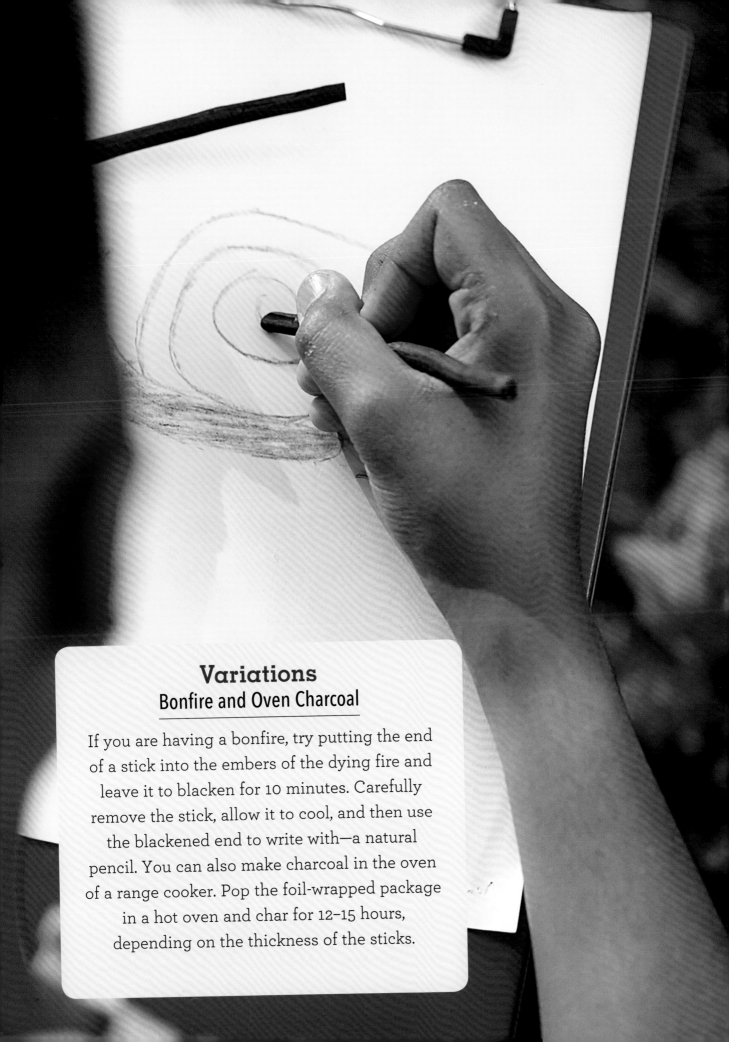

Variations
Bonfire and Oven Charcoal

If you are having a bonfire, try putting the end of a stick into the embers of the dying fire and leave it to blacken for 10 minutes. Carefully remove the stick, allow it to cool, and then use the blackened end to write with—a natural pencil. You can also make charcoal in the oven of a range cooker. Pop the foil-wrapped package in a hot oven and char for 12–15 hours, depending on the thickness of the sticks.

78 Make a Pond Dipping Net

Y-ou can use a net for dipping in ponds and rivers, or in rock pools at the beach. Nets made from natural wood are the best because they don't rust, which can weaken the net at the top. If you are clever, you may find a stick that is pitched like a hayfork (a pitched fork), which you can just slip the net over. This means that you won't have to create a circle of bendy wood. The stick needs to be the right size for the person who is dipping, so hunt carefully for a stick that nature has made to measure for you.

What you need

- ★ An old pair of pantyhose (tights)
- ★ Scissors
- ★ Needle and thread
- ★ A bendy stick (such as willow) or a stick that forks
- ★ Strong string or plastic-coated wire

1 Cut off the legs from the pair of pantyhose (tights) using the scissors.

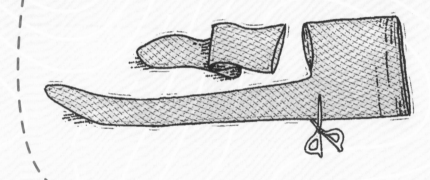

2 Sew up the leg holes using the needle and thread to make your homemade net.

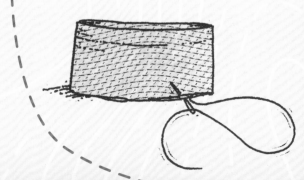

3 Bend the stick to form a loop that you can push your net over. Keep the loop in place by using the string or plastic-coated wire to attach it to the handle of the stick. An extra pair of hands may be needed here to hold the loop steady as you fix it in place.

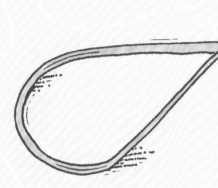

4 Slip the net over the loop or pitched stick (the elastic around the top of the pantyhose will keep it in position) and you have a dipping net.

Tips

★ The dipping net must be strong enough not to bend when you sweep it quickly through water or water plants.

★ If you can't find a long, bendy stick, then make a loop from a wire clothes hanger and attach this to the end of a long, straight stick before slipping over the net.

★ Nylon, or a material with a thin mesh, allows water to pass through quickly. Heavier materials such as cotton won't work because water passes through much too slowly and so your pond dipping won't be such fun.

Spot these Aquatic Plants

Aquatic plants like to grow in or by the edges of rivers and ponds. Green underwater plants often resemble a tropical rainforest, while marsh marigolds and water lilies can be colorful.

Wonderful water lilies There are over 60 varieties of water lily worldwide, and some are very exotic. The Ancient Egyptians even worshipped a water lily called the sacred lotus. White water lilies may look out of place in wild Scottish lochans (or small lakes) or in muddy streams but they are, in fact, a wild flower. The pads of the lilies float like rafts; some leaves are big enough to seat a large group of water-nymph stick people. Smaller leaves may be heart-shaped and provide a perfect float for a more delicate stick fairy. (Turn to page 45 to learn how to make a *Flower Fairy*.) The stems and leaves of water lilies were once considered a delicacy and still are in some countries. Amphibians (i.e. animals that divide their time between water and land) also like eating lily leaves.

During the day the flowers of water lilies float on the surface of the water and, as the sun fades, they close tightly. The water lily pulls in its petals just like a shopkeeper pulls down the shutters of a store at the end of the working day. If, however, you watch a water lily carefully on a dull day, the flower may not bother to open at all. Shopkeepers have to open whatever the weather; water lily flowers are fair-weather flora.

Water lilies are anchored deep under water by firm rhizomes (which are swollen underground stems). In winter the flowers die back and the plants are nourished by food stored in the rhizomes. New stems pop up in the spring. Water lilies are pollinated by insects and, when the lily fruit is ripe, it sinks to the river bed and the seeds pop out and float away to waters new.

Try sketching water lilies with some homemade charcoal (see page 94). If you're interested in capturing finer details, then draw the insects napping on water lily pads. If you sit quietly by a pond, you may hear frogs croaking too.

Duckweed Some water plants such as common or lesser duckweed float at the water's surface. Duckweed is also called duck meat—I'll leave you to work out why. It is one of the smallest pond plants and grows in shallow water because it needs lots of light. Duckweed provides shelter for wildlife, as well as food for many organisms.

Duckweed leaves each produce a new plant—try putting some duckweed in a jar and seeing if it multiplies. A new leaf will grow from a slit in an old leaf. If you like watching pond wildlife, pop some duckweed in a fish tank filled with water to make a plant aquarium. Keep any duckweed under control because otherwise it will stop the plants below getting any light. This is important because plants need light to photosynthesize in order to make food and produce oxygen.

If you put a jar of pond weed in sunshine, you should see bubbles of oxygen. In 1774, a clergyman called Dr Joseph Priestley discovered oxygen while experimenting in a pond in Calne, Wiltshire, England.

80 Make a Waterside Den

If you enjoy studying frogs, make a special den near a pond that has frogspawn and pop back regularly to check up on the developing tadpoles. You could sweep out the den or float a toy raft on the water (see *Make a Toy Raft*, on page 106). You could also leave a tracking tunnel. Cut the ends off a plastic bottle and cover it with black plastic. Pop a piece of white tissue paper and a blob of peanut butter inside the bottle. Place the tunnel in a muddy area—when you return, the bait should have gone and you can study the muddy footprints with your magnifying glass.

Spot this Pond Wildlife

There may be a thousand or more different species living in a small pond or stretch of river, from tiny microscopic creatures to cold-blooded (reptiles) and warm-blooded (mammals) animals.

Dragonfly

Heron

Kingfisher

Otter

Water vole

Leaping salmon

82 Learn to Track

Tracking can be as simple or complicated as you want to make it. You can practice tracking by sprinkling flour or sand from a sandbox on a tray in the garden and seeing which creatures visit. It may be your own pet or a neighbor's cat. On a dry day take a small bag of flour in your wild knapsack and sprinkle it under holes in fences, where it looks as if animals have scampered. Return later and see if you have any wildlife tracks to identify.

Some wild areas and weather conditions are better for tracking wildlife than others. It's easy to spot bird prints on damp sand, at low tide on the seashore. Anywhere were the ground is wet but firms shows tracks up well. Following animal and bird prints in snow is easy because the tracks show clearly. If you go into the garden early in the morning, after snow has fallen, you'll be surprised by the number of paw-shaped (animal) and fork-shaped (bird) tracks that have appeared. A light fall of fresh snow creates the best tracking conditions. Dogs leave pointed tracks, while cats leave rounded paw marks. If deer come into the garden, there may be two-toe-hooved tracks too. In North America there may be antelope or mountain goats. These hoof marks are similar but different to those of deer. Wild boar tracks are hoof-shaped too. In soft ground, you may be able to see claw marks and the webs between toes.

Here are some tracking thoughts and questions to ask:

★ It's easy to spot bird prints on damp sand, at low tide on the seashore. On dry land, however, tracking isn't as easy. Wetlands are a very good place to track birds and other wildlife because the ground is damp. Bogs are not such a good idea, but anywhere where the ground is wet but firm shows tracks up well.

★ Where do the tracks stop? If they stop by a tree, is it a squirrel track? (See if you can spot the difference between a squirrel and hedgehog print.)

★ How close together are the tracks? Was the animal moving quickly or slowly?

★ Look for holes in the ground and at the bottom of trees. Does the hole still house an animal? Have leaves blown into the hole or has there been recent soil disturbance?

★ Look for tracks by puddles. Running through a muddy puddle usually leaves a footprint. You can try this out for yourself.

83 Become a Bone Detective

Animals with backbones are called vertebrates. In mammals, the skeleton is on the inside and acts as a frame on which the body is built. The skeleton grows with the mammal. While you are tracking, look out for bones. Some wildlife is nocturnal and their bones are often the only evidence of their existence. Bone I.D. is challenging, but there is a lot to be learnt from looking at bones. If you find a jaw, for example, the teeth are helpful in species I.D. You can work out if the animal was a herbivore, carnivore, or omnivore (an animal that eats both plants and animals). Age can also be determined—look and see if the teeth are worn. If so, the animal was old. Once you get the basics, you're on the road to becoming a bone detective.

84 Hop on Stepping Stones

Stepping on stones to cross a stream is sensible fun because it means you won't get wet. It's a simple game but you will have to work out the quickest and safest route across the stream, as well as how to shift your balance as you stone hop and jump. If you don't manage to do this, you will get rather damp. As with lots of wild adventures, practice makes perfect.

85 Make Mud Pies

Why not have a mud pie bake-off? Mud pie creations are fun for all age groups. This activity calls for a follow-up swim in a loch, lake, river, or the sea, or perhaps a hot, soapy bath. The buckets and spades will need a good rinse out too.

86 Play Poohsticks

Poohsticks first appeared in A.A. Milne's children's story *The House at Pooh Corner* (1928). Pooh accidentally drops a fir cone in the water and discovers that it reappears on the other side of the bridge. Children use sticks instead of fir cones to play the game. You will need at least two players, a person to be the starter, and a safe bridge to play this game. Younger children should have an adult close by when playing near water.

To play, choose a stick each. Check which way the stream is flowing. The players must face the stream on the side where it flows under the bridge (looking upstream). Each player holds his or her stick at arm's length. The starter should make sure the taller children lower their arms so all the sticks start at the same level. The starter then orders: "On your marks, get set, go!" and the sticks are dropped (not thrown) into the running water. The players rush across the bridge to the other side to see which stick comes through first. The winner is the owner of the first stick under the bridge.

87 Skim Stones

This traditional game is best played on a sunny windless day. The idea is simple: hold a flat stone between your finger and thumb and throw it onto water so it skims the surface as many times as possible before finally sinking. To play, pick a stone that is as thin and light as possible. Throw the stone with as much force as you can, as horizontally as possible, and from as low to the ground as you can bend, while ensuring that you are still able to swing your arm to throw. The key to a good throw is to spin the stone.

88 Make a Toy Raft

You can have lots of fun sailing a toy raft in streams and ponds. You can build a simple wooden raft or attach a separate mast and sail as well if you wish. You will need to cut some sticks or small branches to make the base of the raft using a pair of hand pruners (secateurs).

What you need

★ 20 thick sticks or small branches (of an even thickness), measuring 9–12in (23–30cm) in length

★ String

★ Scissors

★ Corks (optional)

1 Choose the two thickest sticks to act as support sticks. Take the first of these support sticks and attach a length of string, about ½in (1cm) or so from one end of the stick. Put the other support stick to one side.

2 Tie the first of your remaining sticks to the first support stick. (You don't need to use knots—just wrap the string tightly on both sides of the support stick in a continuous figure-of-eight pattern.)

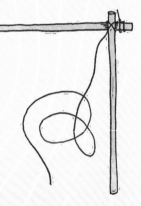

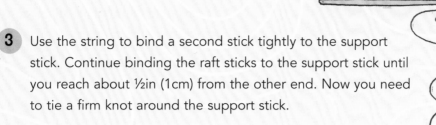

3 Use the string to bind a second stick tightly to the support stick. Continue binding the raft sticks to the support stick until you reach about ½in (1cm) from the other end. Now you need to tie a firm knot around the support stick.

4 With all of the raft sticks attached to the first support stick, you should now have only the second support stick remaining. Take this stick and start tying the other end of all the raft sticks to it in the same way as you did for the first support stick. Keep the string as tight as you can, weaving it in and out of the sticks as you bind them securely to the second support stick. When you have finished, tie a firm knot and cut the string. You now have a simple but useful toy raft.

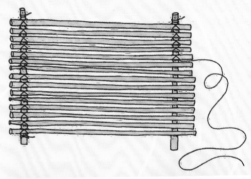

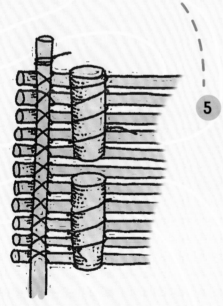

5 If your raft needs help to float, tie some corks to the side or underneath. Tie a long piece of string to make a tether to stop your raft floating away.

Adding a Mast and Sail
If you wish, you can make a mast and sail for your raft. Use a straight stick for the mast and weave the sail using long, flat leaves, such as iris leaves or reeds, and attach it to two support sticks.

89 Grow Your Own Mistletoe

Mistletoe seeds are spread by birds, but young naturalists can have a go at seeding mistletoe too. Mistletoe has interesting interactions with some insects, birds, mammals, and fungi, as well as the host tree on which it grows. In fact, it forms its own mini ecosystem. In the United Kingdom, the aptly named mistle thrush gets its common name from its love of mistletoe berries. In North America the botanical name for mistletoe is *Phoradendron*, which comes from the Greek words "thief" and "tree." This is clever because mistletoe is a parasite and hitchhikes a ride on the host tree—it's a tree thief.

To seed mistletoe, push the sticky seeds from the white berries as far as you can into the bark of a tree in your garden or a local wild tree. Mistletoe seeds are naturally sticky. Be patient. Fingers crossed that you will know where to find mistletoe in the years to come. The more berries you can find to do this with, the greater your chance of success. Always wash your hands after seeding mistletoe.

90 Make a Bug House

Arrange three to four small, clean, recycled food containers in a shoebox or a small box with a lid. Fill each half of the containers with a different habitat, e.g. white and black shredded paper, dry and wet leaves, wet and dry moss, damp bark, dry grass, and dry and wet soil. Catch a few tiny insects that don't jump—woodlice are ideal—and pop them in the box. Make some holes in the lid of the box with a screwdriver or tapestry needle, and leave the woodlice to choose their favorite home. Come back in an hour or two and see which homes the woodlice have chosen.

91 Make a Bird-Feeding Roll

In late summer and fall (autumn), try gathering as many different berries, fruits, nuts, and seeds as you can to make a special garden feeder for birds. You can also dry the seeds and store them in envelopes before sowing them in a wild garden in spring. Some very fine seeds are swept away by the wind, but others are eaten or buried by wildlife. This is how plants seed themselves in different places. After Hallowe'en, you might also like to attach a strong hanging loop to your pumpkin or swede lantern and use it as a bird feeder.

What you need

★ 2–3 handfuls of wild fall (autumn) berries and fruits (e.g. haws, hips, rowan berries, sloes, and elderberries)

★ Large handful of wild seeds and nuts

★ Small tray

★ Scissors

★ Empty cardboard tube (such as kitchen or toilet paper roll)

★ 2 thin, straight twigs, about 6in (15cm) in length and no more than ½in (1cm) thick

★ Table knife

★ Jar of smooth peanut butter or coconut oil

1 Put the berries, fruits, nuts, and seeds on a small tray.

2 Use the scissors to make two tiny snips opposite each other at each end of the cardboard tube (about ¾in/2cm from the ends). That makes four snips in total.

3 Gently push a twig through the opposite holes so that there is an equal amount of twig poking out on each side of the cardboard tube.

4 Tie a length of string to the end of each twig and then tie the opposite strings together to make two hanging loops.

5 Use the knife to spread a thin layer of peanut butter over the tube and then carefully roll this in the berries, fruits, nuts, and seeds. You may need to use your finger to gently push larger seeds and berries into the peanut butter. Make sure the string doesn't get stuck to the tube.

6 Hang the roll from a branch or bird table near a window. Then watch the birds snacking on the wild food you've provided. You could also stick some clumps of light seeds (e.g. dock or sorrel) to the tube, but make sure they aren't too heavy or they will fall off.

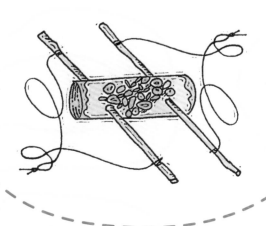

Try this too!

Look for some big fir cones in the woods. Don't worry if they are damp and tightly shut; left to sunbathe, the cones will open up. Tie a length of strong string around the top of the fir cone and make a hanging loop. Push lashings of coconut oil, lard, or peanut butter into the gaps in the open cone and then push wild seeds and berries into the fat—this is messy but fun. Hang the cones on a branch and keep watch for feathered visitors.

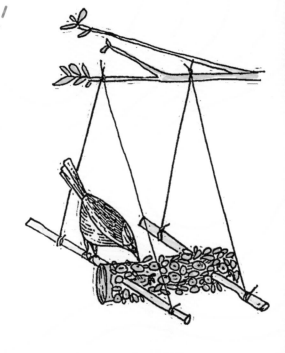

92 Make an Iced Feeding Basket

In the fall (autumn), you can collect hips, haws, seeds, and nuts to freeze and then feed them to the hungry birds in winter. If you also add some colorful leaves to your sphere of wildness, you'll remember the pretty colors of fall as the ice slowly melts on a winter's day.

What you need

★ Small bowl

★ Orange or lemon (fruit) net

★ Berries, hips, haws, small pieces of cone, nuts, and seeds

★ Colorful leaves (optional)

★ Water

★ Piece of string, about 20in (50cm) in length

★ Large bowl of warm water

1　Line the small bowl with the unopened end of the fruit net. The bowl needs to be small enough for the net to cover the inside and leave 2–2¼in (5–6cm) hanging over the rim.

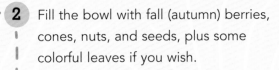

2　Fill the bowl with fall (autumn) berries, cones, nuts, and seeds, plus some colorful leaves if you wish.

3 Pour some water into the bowl until it's three-quarters full. As water freezes, its properties change and it takes up more space—a sneaky science lesson. If you fill the bowl to the brim with water, it may crack as the water expands.

4 Pop the bowl in the freezer for 2–3 hours or until it has frozen.

5 Remove the bowl from the freezer. Grasp the edge of the netting and use the string to tie it tightly together. Make sure you have secured the netting well and that the length of string is long enough to hang the ball from a tree.

6 Quickly pop the bowl in and out of a large bowl of warm water—this will loosen the netting from the sides of the smaller bowl.

7 Lift the frozen ball out of the bowl and pop it back in the freezer until you are ready to hang it from a tree.

Variation
Frozen Berry Cubes

You can also freeze some berries with a little water in an ice-cube tray. To feed the birds out of season, put the berry ice cubes on a winter bird table.

93 Make Wild Flower Water

Collect a small basket of rose or gorse petals. Place the petals in a saucepan and add just enough water to cover them. Warm the water over a low heat. Don't let the water boil (lots of big, fast bubbles), but simmer (tiny bubbles) for about 45 minutes until the petals lose their color. Cover the pan with a lid and leave the water to cool. Strain the scented water through a sieve into a pitcher (jug) and then pour into a clean screw-top bottle or jar. Label your wild flower water and store it in the refrigerator.

When you're hot, you can cool yourself down by splashing a little rosewater on your wrists or face. You can also freeze the rose petals to capture the roses' scent. You could make some rosewater in winter, which would bring back lovely summer memories whenever you open the bottle.

TIP
Shake the petals well after you've picked them to ensure any visiting insects don't end up in your flower water.

94 Make a Cobweb Card

A clever photographer snaps a cobweb while it's still coated in dew or rain drops. Very early in the morning (after you've run barefoot through the dew) is a brilliant time for you to try to do this. Later in the day you could spray a cobweb with water instead, and then take a photograph. Spiders' webs can look hauntingly beautiful on foggy fall (autumn) mornings. This project traps a real spider's web on a piece of card. Remember that a small creature has made the web so it's not kind to do this often.

Find a silky spider's web without a spider or any of its food (prey) trapped in the web. Hold a piece of white card (measuring about 6 x 6in/15 x 15cm) behind the web and use a pair of tweezers to carefully pull the web into the center of the card. Spray the card with hairspray and leave to dry.

95 Make a Bug Attractor

Bugs are attracted to sugar and this rather messy activity will allow you to look at them with a magnifying glass. In a small bowl mix a ripe banana with a little brown sugar and leave it for 20 minutes. Find a small log or branch and then smear this with the banana mix. Check up on your experiment a little later to see if there are any visiting insects. Avoid insects that may sting but, if you want to inspect one more carefully, scoop it up with an old spoon and pop it in a glass jar with a bottle cap of water, a stick, and some juicy green leaves. Put the lid on the jar or use some baking parchment secured with a rubber band. Use a fork to poke some holes through the jar cover to ensure the insect has fresh air. Don't keep an insect prisoner for very long and release it where you found it.

96 Have a Gastropod Race

First prepare a racetrack by spraying a tray or plate with some water to help the snails to glide. Use a twig or pen to mark the start and finish lines. Find two snails. Squish some berry juice over one shell so you can tell the snails apart. If you have more than two snails racing, then you could mark the shells with numbered stickers. Set the snails at the start line and wait—the race will take place at a snail's pace. You might want to entice your snails to the finish line with some chickweed. Look out for slimy tracks.

TIPS

- Snails like damp, shady places. Look for them under plant pots, along the sides of rotting wood, at the base of walls, and under large leaves.

- Snails have a homing instinct, which means that crafty gardeners who throw snails into a neighbor's garden may find that the same snails return to eat their plants instead.

- Finding snails isn't always easy. If you keep your snails for more than 24 hours, make sure that the soil is damp and feed them fresh greenery such as grasses, chickweed, or dandelion leaves.

97 Build a Snail Hotel

Find a clear plastic bottle with a screw top and cut a small rectangular opening on one side of the bottle (make cuts on three sides and leave the door hinge intact). Make air holes with a fork. Fill the bottle base (on the opposite side of the door) with damp soil and fresh greenery. Put a snail (or two if you are using a large bottle) inside the hotel, close the door (with tape if necessary), and watch for a day or two. Remember to release the snail back into the wild.

98 Build a Wormery

A worm changes the structure of its environment by creating burrows through which water and oxygen can enter and carbon dioxide leave the soil. Charles Darwin called worms "Nature's Ploughs" because they mix soil and organic matter.

What you need

★ Large glass jar or plastic bottle

★ Precision screwdriver or tapestry needle

★ 2 circles of wax (greaseproof) paper (to cover the jar or bottle)

★ Small square of newspaper

★ Water spray

★ Sand, leaves, and moist soil (to fill the wormery)

★ Earthworm

★ Vegetable and fruit peelings, tea leaves, coffee grindings, and salad or wild leaves

★ Rubber bands

★ Black paper and sticky tape

1. If you are using a plastic bottle, cut away the neck and poke 5–6 holes in the bottom using the small screwdriver or tapestry needle. Use the screwdriver or needle to make a few small holes in the circles of wax (greaseproof) paper too.

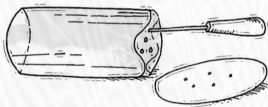

2. Tear the newspaper into small pieces, spray them with water, and use them to line the bottom of the jar or bottle.

3 Add a layer of sand, followed by a layer of leaves, and then a layer of moist soil. Continue layering in this way until you are within 2¼in (6cm) of the top of the jar or bottle.

4 Dig up an earthworm. Have a good look at your worm and then pop it in the wormery.

5 Put some food such as vegetable and fruit peelings in the jar or bottle, cover the opening with the circles of wax (greaseproof) paper, and then secure with the rubber bands.

6 Wrap some black paper around the jar or bottle and keep it in place with some sticky tape. (You can also cover the wormery with a lightweight blanket if this is easier.)

7 Place the wormery in a cool, dark place and check each day to see what your earthworm is up to—you'll need to remove the black paper to do this.

8 Release the captive earthworm into the wild when you have studied the patterns it makes in the soil.

99 Go Star-Gazing

There are 88 official constellations. Check them out one at a time—different constellations appear in the night sky throughout the year.

Find Orion and Cassiopeia Today, we still use the names given to the constellations by Ptolemy. Orion is a constellation named after a mythological Greek hunter. Lots of stars make up Orion's shape. Rigel, the brightest star, is found in one of the hunter's legs. One of the easiest of Ptolemy's constellations to spot is Cassiopeia, which is named after the boastful, vain queen from Greek mythology. This constellation is visible all year round in the Northern Hemisphere and its bright stars make the shape of the letter "W."

Find the Big Dipper The Big Dipper (USA) or The Plough (UK) is easy to identify: it's a group of seven stars and is a good place to begin your star-gazing adventures. The Big Dipper is an asterism, which is part of the constellation Ursa Major. In Latin this means Greater She Bear. According to Native American legend, Ursa Major is lowest in the sky when the bear is looking for a place to lie down for its winter hibernation, and highest in the spring.

To join the Roman army, soldiers had to take an eye test that involved spotting stars in the handle of the Big Dipper. If a Roman solider could spot Alcor, which is brighter than Mizar, he passed the test to serve as an archer. Dubhe and Merak, the two outermost stars of the Big Dipper, point to The North Star or Polaris. Amateur astronomers call these stars the pointers—if you extend a line about six times the distance between Dubhe and Merak and can't see a bright star, the North Star, you've not found the Big Dipper. the Plough or Big Dipper rotates counterclockwise around the North Star, which means it can appear "upside down" or "sideways" on. Some people call this group of stars the saucepan. This asterism appears on the Cherokee peace flag and Alaska state flag.

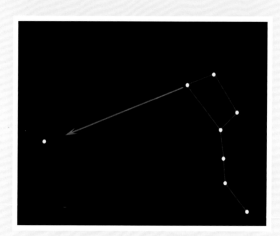

Find the North Star This star sits above the North Pole and is the only star that doesn't move—other stars circle around it. True north lies directly under this star—in times of old, sailors used this star to chart their direction of sail. When you spend time star- and moon-gazing, you too can be guided by nature. Natural navigation is not only out-of-door fun but useful too.

TIPS

- Big starry skies are best viewed far away from the glare of streetlights in cities and towns, which can cause light pollution. You can check on a dark sky website to find the best local place to star-gaze, but a dark back garden or local park is often a good place to start. You can, of course, see stars with the naked eye in cities, but you'll get a better view if you go further from street lighting.

- Winter is a good time for family constellation viewing because the sun sets early. You may even be lucky enough to see a meteor (shooting star) or the brighter planets: Jupiter, Mars, and Venus. Venus is the brightest star in the Solar System and can be seen during the day if you know where to look. When Venus is to the west of the Sun, she rises before the Sun and is known as the Morning Star. When Venus is to the east, she shines just after sunset, and is then called the Evening Star.

100 Go Moon-Watching

On a clear night you can see the Moon with your naked eye. The Moon controls the oceans and rules over the tides. You'll notice the Moon's power when the sea races over the sand and destroys your sandcastles. Neil Armstrong was the first man to step on the Moon on July 21, 1969. Only twelve people have set foot on the Moon and their footprints are still there. We can still see these footprints because, unlike the Earth, the Moon has no atmosphere. If you look at the surface of the Moon through binoculars, you may see craters, pits, and scars caused by large pieces of rock hitting its surface billons of years ago.

101 Host a Moths' Dinner Party

Loop a strong rubber band around the center of a tennis ball so it is taut. Tie one end of a 40-in (100-cm) length of craft string to the rubber band. Loop the length and secure with a knot so that the ball can hang from the string. Over a low heat, warm ¾ cup (200ml) of fruit juice and 3 tablespoons of brown sugar in a small pan until the sugar dissolves. Carefully pour the syrupy mixture into a small bowl and pop in the ball. Leave the ball to soak for 15 minutes, turning it occasionally to ensure it is well coated. Take the bowl into the garden (to avoid sticky drips) and hang the ball in a sheltered place in a tree or bush—watch out for night-time visitors.

Soak five or six 10–20in (25–50cm) lengths of rag in the fruit syrup (as above). Squeeze out the excess syrup and pop the strips on a tray. Peg the strips on a washing line or hang them over the branches of a tree. Wait until after dark and check which species of moths have invited themselves to dine at your moths' dinner party. You can also use a pastry brush to paint the syrupy mixture onto the bark of a garden tree.

Resources

Foraging and the Law

As a forager, you need to learn about the ingredients yourself; there isn't a short cut. Laws differ from country to country and can change from time to time, so please check local regulations before you start. The following websites may be useful:

UK (not Scotland)
http://www.legislation.gov.uk/ukpga/1968/60/contents

Theft Act 1968
"A person who picks mushrooms growing wild on any land, or who picks flowers, fruit or foliage from a plant growing wild on any land, does not (although not in possession of the land) steal what he picks, unless he does it for reward, or for sale, or other commercial purpose."

Be aware of by-laws, which, in places, may remove foraging rights.

National Association forEnvironmental Education (UK)
http://www.nationalrural.org/organisation.aspx?id=caeafb14-5fac-42a0-9904-05cd911eb257

SCOTLAND
http://www.snh.gov.uk/enjoying-the-outdoors/your-access-rights

US
US laws regarding foraging vary at the federal, state, and city levels, and certain parks also have their own rules. Foragers in Texas should pay particular attention to state laws.

United States Environmental Protection Agency
http://www.epa.gov/lawsregs/policy/

North American Association for Environmental Education
http://www.naaee.net/

CANADA
www.gov.mb.ca/conservation/firstnations/hunting_fishing_oct_09.pdf

The Natural Resources Transfer Agreement (NRTA), which forms part of the Constitution Act, 1930, provides that Indian people "have the right, which the Province hereby assures to them, of hunting, trapping and fishing game and fish for food at all seasons of the year on all unoccupied Crown lands and on any other lands to which (they) may have a right of access." Treaty and Aboriginal rights relating to hunting, fishing and gathering are also recognized and affirmed as part of the Constitution of Canada by Section 35 of the Constitution Act, 1982.

Useful Websites

American Museum of Natural History
http://www.amnh.org

Attenborough Nature Reserve
http://www.attenboroughnaturecentre.co.uk

Audubon Society (Birds USA)
http://www.audubon.org

Bat Conservation International
http://www.batcon.org

Beatrix Potter
http://www.bpotter.com

Boy Scouts of America
http://www.scouting.org

Bumblebee Conservation Trust
http://www.bumblebeeconservation.org

Bushcraft
* http://www.bushcraftUK.com (UK)
* http://www.bushcraftusa.com (USA)

Disabled Access
* http://www.accessibleguide.co.uk/home.php (UK)
* http://www.euansguide.com (UK)
* http://www.wheelyboats.org (UK)
* http://www.whizz-kidz.org.uk (UK)
* http://www.disabilityresources.org/PARENTS-OF.html (USA)
* http://www.easterseals.com (USA)

Earth's Endangered Creatures
http://www.earthsendangered.com/index.asp

Eilean Bàn (The Bright Water Centre)
http://www.eileanban.org

Geocaching
http://www.geocaching.com

Ghost Fishing
http://www.ghostfishing.org

Girlguiding
http://www.girlguiding.org.uk

Girl Scouts of America
http://www.girlscouts.org

Healthy Seas
http://www.healthyseas.org

International Dark-Sky Association (IDA)
http://www.darksky.org

Jake's Bones
http://www.jakes-bones.com

John Muir Trust
https://www.johnmuirtrust.org

Jurassic Coast World Heritage Site
http://www.jurassiccoast.org

Marine Conservation Society
http://www.mcsuk.org

MarLIN The Marine Life Information Network
http://www.marlin.ac.uk/index.php

Moon Phases (Northern and Southern Hemispheres)
http://www.moonconnection.com

National Geographic Kids
http://www.ngkids.co.uk

The National Trust
http://www.nationaltrust.org.uk

Natural History Museum
http://www.nhm.ac.uk

North American Mycological Association
http://www.namyco.org

The Plastic Bank
http://www.plasticbank.org

Project Seagrass
http://www.projectseagrass.org

Rachel Carson
http://www.rachelcarson.org

The Royal Society for the Protection of Birds
http://www.rspb.org.uk

The Scout Association (UK)
http://www.scouts.org.uk

Sierra Club
http://www.sierraclub.org

Slow Food
http://www.slowfood.com

The Society for the Preservation of Natural History Collections (including preserving seaweed)
http://www.spnhc.org

The Wild Network
http://www.thewildnetwork.com

The Wildlife Trusts
http://www.wildlifetrusts.org

World Wildlife Fund
http://www.worldwildlife.org

WoRMS World Register of Marine Species
http://www.marinespecies.org

The WWW Virtual Library: Mycology
http://www.mycology.cornell.edu

UK Courses
* http://www.eatweeds.co.uk/about
* http://www.forageireland.com
* https://www.forestschools.com
* http://www.gallowaywildfoods.com (foraging)
* http://www.shadowhawk.co.uk (tracking)
* http://www.wildaboutpembrokeshire.co.uk (foraging)

US courses and Books

http://www.foraging.com

Books to Read

A Fruit Is a Suitcase for Seeds by Jean Richards
A Home for Hermit Crab by Eric Carle
A Seed Is Sleepy by Dianna Hutts Aston
Animal Skulls—A Guide to North American Species by Mark Elbroch
Bat Loves the Night by Nicola Davies
Berries, Nuts and Seeds by Diane L. Burns
Flip, Float, Fly!: Seeds on the Move by JoAnn Early Macken
Flower Fairy Series by Cecily Mary Barker
From Seed to Maple Tree: Following the Life Cycle by Laura Purdie Salas
Growing Frogs by Vivian French
Hiding in the Woods: A Nature Trail Book by Maurice Pledger
How a Seed Grows by Helene J. Jordon
Kildee House by Rutherford George Montgomery
Language of Flowers by Kate Greenaway
Little House in the Big Woods by Laura Ingalls Wilder
Lobo the Wolf: King of the Currumpaw by Ernest Thompson Seton
Lost in the Barrens by Farley Mowat
Madam How and Lady Why by Charles Kingsley
My Favorite Tree: Terrific Trees of North America by Diane Iverson
My Side of the Mountain by Jean Craighead George

My Wild Wild Kitchen by Jean Craighead George
Paddle-to-the-Sea by Holling C. Holling
Parables From Nature by Mrs. Alfred Gatty
Ring of Bright Water by Gavin Maxwell
Tarka the Otter by Henry Williamson
The Bramley Hedge Series by Jill Barklem
The Dandelion Seed by Joseph Anthony
The Tale of Peter Rabbit (and later books) by Beatrix Potter
The Water Babies by Charles Kingsley
The Wind in the Willows by Kenneth Graham
The Yearling by Marjorie Rawlings
Watership Down by Richard Adams
We're Going on a Bear Hunt by Michael Rosen and Helen Oxenbury

Books for parents

A selection of good reference books for accurate identification of plants and animals will prove useful.
A Guide to Wild Edible Plants for Parents, Grandparents, and Teachers to Use with Children by Steve Brill
The Sense of Wonder by Rachel Carson

Some Wild Apps

BirdLog
BudBurst
Forestry Commission (cellphone/ mobile apps)
Meteor Counter
Project Noah
What's Invasive
Wild Time (Project Wild Thing)

Some geocaching Apps
http://www.notaboutthenumbers.com/2012/05/11/top-5-android-geocaching-apps/

Index

Picture credits

Key t—top; m—middle; b—bottom; l—left; r—right

All photography by Dylan Drummond except for:

Barbara Olive p.17b

Claire Richardson pp.28l, 84,

David Merewether pp.23tr, 55ml

Debbie Patterson pp.22l, 23tl,

Gavin Kingcome pp.118, 122,

Gloria Nicol (Rosehip) p.57

Peter Moore pp.54br, 55b, 55t,

Polly Wreford pp.14bl, 54tr, 66tl,

Terry Benson pp.2, 10, 16t, 33–34, 61, 69, 95, 109–111, 116–117, 121, 123

Getty Images/
Alex Treadway (background) p.101; Andrey Nekrasov (squid) p.81br; Andy Roberts p.56; Anne Vornbrock/Eye Em p.48; Anthony Lee p.67m; Anthony Spencer Photography p.23m; Arturo de Frias Photography (stag) p.43b; BHS (whelk) p.81tl; Bob Bennett (beaver) p.1r, p.101bl; Brasil2 (scallops) p.81bl; Christopher Hope-Fitch p.21b, p.38; Daniel Walls/Eye Em p.67b; Dave Greenwood p.35; David Courtenay (Bumble Bee) p.54l; David J Slater p.23br; David Tipling p.26t (vole) p.43ml; Dennie Cody/Duangkamon Khattiya p.21t; Flavia Morlachetti p.20l; James Warwick (Kingfisher) p.101ml; Jessica Lee/EyeEm (rabbit) p.43mr; Jim Cumming (fox) p.42b, p.103; Joe Cornish (mussels) p.81tr; Jon Boyes (limpets) p.80tr; Kevin Oke (crab) p.80b; Kumacore p.99; Les Stocker (bat) p.43t; Louise Heusinkveld (Otter) p.101mr; Marlou Gaurano/Eye Em p.66b; Mary C. Legg (mayfly) p.101tl; MASAFUMI KIMURA/a. collectionRF p.22r; Michael Marsh/Stocks Images p.66tr; Michael Miller/Eye Em p.20r; Mike Powles (dormouse) p.42tl; Otto Stadler p.102; Paul Kay (periwinkle) p.71ml; Paul Tourlonias/Eye Em p.39b, (woodpecker) p.42tr; Peter Muller p.17t; Pixedeli p.47; R A Kearton (barnacles) p.81ml; Reinhard Dirscherl (octopus) p.81mr; Robin Bush (background) pp.54–55; Sandra Sandbridge (heron) p.101tr; Sara Standbridge p.67t; Sean Gallup p.86b; Thomas Kitchin & Victoria Hurst/Design Pics (leaping salmon) p.101br; Tonpicknick (cockles) p.80ml; ullstein bild (starfish) p.71tr; Vishal Poorswani/Eye Em p.70; Walter Bibikow (oysters) p.80mr

iStock/
p.13tr & p.100 iStock/kikkerdirk (yellow frog)

Shutterstock/
Mike Charles pp.71 (background), pp.80–81 (background)

South12th Photography p.86t